W9-CFK-946

After wandering among Helen's bavarian buildings and perhaps enjoying the revelry of Oktoberfest, many visitors naturally ask how Helen became **"Georgia's Alpine Village"**. There's a tale behind the architecture, of course, and it is recounted here. And from even earlier times, little remains in modern Helen to suggest that Main Street follows the route of an ancient Indian trading path, that pioneers once labored here to claim fields from a mountain wilderness, or that the shrieking whistles of trains and the belching smokestacks of a huge sawmill shaped valley life in an age of steam. Although the great Georgia Gold Rush overturned the valley floors and left scars on the surrounding hillsides, it's not generally recognized that the Helen area saw as much prospecting and speculation as any other part of the Georgia gold region. Together, these events are the *Story of Helen*.

There are a lot of interesting things in the Helen area as well. Readers will find information and history on these sites listed on the opposing map:

The Story of HELEN
and THEREABOUTS

By Matt Gedney

Published by: *Little Star Press*
  175 Mt. Calvary Road
  Marietta, GA 30064 U.S.A.

All rights reserved. No part of this book may be reproduced or transmitted in any form or by any means, electronic or mechanical, including photocopying, recording or by any information storage or retrieval system without written permission from the author, except for the inclusion of brief quotations in a review.

Copyright © 1998 by Matt Gedney
Cover by Cindy Gedney and David Greear
"Rafter's Rush" on cover © 1997 by Donna Myers
"Fantasy Lane" on page 13 and cover © 1997 by Donna Myers
"Movie Funeral Scene" on page 14 and cover © 1998 by Ken Woodall
First Printing 1998
10 9 8 7 6 5 4 3 2 1

Printed in the United States of America

Publisher's Cataloging in Publication Data
Gedney, Matthias J.
The Story of Helen and Thereabouts: by Matt Gedney -- First Edition
 88 p. 23cm.
1. Helen (Georgia) -- History
2. Georgia Mountains -- Travel Guide

1998 LCC 98-91220
ISBN 0-9651196-8-8: $8.95 Softcover

CONTENTS

EARLY BALLOONIST. *Looking like a scene from the* Wizard of Oz, *an early Alpine aviator rises over the original downtown area of Helen in 1974.*

In a scene typical of Alpine Helen's early days, long-time resident
Warren Brown drives one of his prized antique cars in an Alpine parade.

CHAPTER 1: AN ALPINE TALE

*T*HE HELEN VALLEY has an interesting history which includes Indians,
pioneers, gold fever and the creation of the town itself when it was selected
as the site of the largest band sawmill in Georgia, but it's the story of how Helen
became "Georgia's Alpine Village" which most likely arouses the curiosity of
the first-time visitor.

Helen had gotten off to a roaring start as a sawmill town way back in
1913, when the trains of the Gainesville and Northwestern Railroad steamed
into the valley. Times were good as long as the big sawmill and the railroad
were there, but things got tough when both left about the time the Great Depression set in. In the years after World War II, Helen's commercial fortunes improved when Jimmy Wilkins moved up from the Buckhead section of Atlanta to
operate a small hosiery mill in the 40s and 50s. In the early 1960s, Wilkins
founded Orbit Manufacturing Company, a larger enterprise which manufactured ladies apparel and was a mainstay of the community for 35 years.

***At the Ice-Burg Drive-In**, as Lee Abernathy put it, you could get "hamburgers with slaw, french fries with slaw, and slaw with slaw". When it became the Wurst Haus, you got sauerkraut.*

And when the town voted to sell beer and wine, it was the only place for miles where alcohol could be bought legally. Even though legality had never been much of a problem in obtaining something to drink in the mountains, the move was immediately successful. Helen's several restaurants thrived and package sales were good, soon yielding enough in taxes to build a much-needed city hall. Business got even better when package sales of liquor were approved a few years later.

During its first six decades, Helen became a close-knit community, home to a mixture of local mountaineers and a diverse group who collected from more distant points to work at one of the mills or just to enjoy urban life in the mountains. Story-tellers occupied the "loafers benches" around town, everybody pretty much knew everyone else, gleeful children were free to roam the uncrowded valley, and most of the town would turn out when somebody died. The government built three housing projects during the Great Society years, bringing Helen's population to about 250 during the 1960s.

However, by the late 1960s, the old downtown area had taken on a run-down appearance. It hadn't grown much for years; a number of the aging buildings were vacant and almost all were in need of at least a coat of paint. Stores had come and gone as local shoppers took advantage of better roads to do most of their buying at larger retail centers about a half-hour away.

Helen once had a large resort hotel which succeeded in attracting a number of guests, but it had burned 25 years before. Now, except for overnight stays in the small Chattahoochee Motel at the upper end of town and the several outlet stores, tourists stopped only for necessities, beer (a necessity for some) or to eat at one of the two restaurants, since this was all the town had to offer.

The drugstore, post office, Warren Brown's Gas and Groceries and Chief's Garage were mainstays; the coin-operated "Laun-Dry-Eze" laundry, the "Ice-Berg" hamburger joint, Charlie Maloof's business office and a couple of outlet stores completed the downtown scene. Across the Chattahoochee River, the large plate glass windows of the Mountain Air Restaurant surveyed this peaceful but less-than-thriving vista. On an early January day in 1969, beside these large glass windows, the process which led to Helen's Alpine conversion began. It didn't take long.

Among those having lunch at the Mountain Air that day were Jimmy Wilkins, owner of Orbit Manufacturing and several downtown buildings where his hosiery mill had been, and Pete Hodkinson, whose several business interests included outlet stores for Orbit products. At lunch, the remark was made that something should be done to spruce up the town. The next move was Pete's: he talked with artist John Kollock, then a week-end resident of nearby Clarkesville who, like himself, attended the Episcopal Church there.

It was Kollock's notion that put a face and a name on the renovation of downtown Helen. Kollock envisioned an "Alpine Village" with storefronts reminiscent of buildings he had seen as a young soldier in the Bavarian region of Germany. After wandering about town photographing the fading buildings , he returned to the studio and in less than a week produced a set of colorful sketches showing the possibilities if red roofs, white stucco, and fancy trim were applied over the concrete blocks, aging wood and weathered bricks of old Helen.

Kollock didn't look for much of a response, but he didn't expect the decisiveness of Jimmy Wilkins, who immediately endorsed the idea, as did the city council. There were doubts at first about whether everyone would sign up, but all of the downtown business owners soon agreed to convert their buildings. This surprising display of cooperation was especially notable since several owners had little expectation of much profit from tourists and some had to take out sizeable loans.

Thus, in only a few short weeks, all of the necessary pieces were in place. With the initiative of Pete Hodkinson, the handy notion of John Kollock, the decisiveness and financial support of Jimmy Wilkins, and the unanimous participation of local businessmen like Warren Brown, Chief Westmoreland, J.S. Chastain, Dot Watson and Charlie Maloof, the Alpine enterprise was ready to go forward.

Artist John Kollock watches as "perennial promoter" Pete Hodkinson prepares to toast a ground-breaking.

Working only from Kollock's sketches, local builders J.S. Chastain and Roy Sims were busy on the first buildings less than a month after the idea of a renovation was first discussed at the Mountain Air Restaurant. As Roy put it, "I don't know the difference between a Swiss Chalet and a geisha house, but we'll do it!"

Things did not slow after the fast start. Most of the old downtown buildings were converted before 1969 was over. The next year saw finishing touches applied as power and phone lines were moved and placed underground. The phone company installed two bavarian-themed phone booths, proclaiming them to be "probably the only ones of their kind in the country". The city converted the site of a former gas station in the center of town into a small park. Kollock went about painting scenes of local history on the fresh, white Bavarian stucco.

Success came quickly. As something new in the mountains, the town became a magnet for reporters and throngs of tourists who followed close behind. Helen made a great story: a small town, without any government help, remakes itself in record time in a remarkable display of civic cooperation. New buildings were soon growing beside the remodeled old ones; the number of downtown businesses tripled in three years. Helen won many awards from the "Stay and See Georgia" program and other organizations. Delegations from other small towns came to study Helen's "minor miracle".

However, the locals were about as surprised as anyone by the degree of Alpine success. As Helen experienced growing pains, the city government was re-organized, parking lots were established and a Chamber of Commerce formed. Traditional residents began leaving town, usually with a good profit from the sale of the old homeplace if they happened to own it. Beautification programs added details like flowers and Alpine trash cans. Street dances with country music were abandoned in favor of the Oktoberfest event which became an annual ritual. Helen had relied on septic tanks, but was forced to build a sewage treatment plant big enough to handle the contributions of thousands of visitors.

Many people put a lot of effort into the early development of the Alpine Village; among them were mayors Haine Sims, "Crosstie" Palmer, and Bob Fowler, Chamber of Commerce President Ola Adams Masters, and town publicist and photographer Bernd Nagy who founded the House of Tyrol. However, for seven years, Pete Hodkinson III was the essential Alpine man.

A charismatic figure with a penchant for risk and a flair for promotion, Pete put all of his energies into the Alpine Village. He declared Helen a refuge

After the original buildings were remodeled, *power and phone lines were moved (including the string of Christmas lights). The city constructed a small park as a centerpiece, which has since been enlarged to take in the parking area in front of the stores. The remodeled phone booth was described as "probably the only Alpine phone booth in the State". Except for another one in Helen, it probably still is.*

of "free spirits", and in his vicinity it was a haven where spirits of the more usual liquid kind often flowed freely. As head of the Alpine Valley Investment Corporation, Pete found financing hard to come by but always had a vision for the town. Ideas, some of them wild and eccentric, swirled about.

Pete also gave voice to a unique brand of what might be called "Alpine Idealism". Helen would remain true to its alpine theme. Businesses would be operated by their proprietors, motel owners would live on the premises. Franchises would not be allowed, nor would competition -- there would be only one of each kind of shop. Going a step further, Pete vowed to remove any item from his own shop if he learned it was also sold in an Atlanta store. Helen would not become a tacky tourist trap or "be like Gatlinburg". The locally-run Investment Corporation would maintain control by buying up all the property and selling only to buyers who would go along with the plan.

Following the "European small-town model", Helen would preserve green space around the business district. By 1976, Pete was working on a 36-hole golf course to fill the green space below town; a flag fluttered over a solitary green, which needed only a fairway to complete the first link in his visionary scene. A theater to house "The Sound of Music" and other attractions was under construction. The first trolley car of the "Helen Transit Authority" neared completion to await the installation of rails for carrying tourists into the shopping district from new parking lots to be located beyond the golf course at the lower end of the valley.

Pete's vision would not be realized. Two years before, this "perennial promoter" had brought hot-air ballooning to Helen. With great fanfare, the "Helen-to-the-Atlantic" balloon race had been organized. Described by Pete with the usual drama as the "race from the center of the earth to the edge of the world", he even got Fortune Magazine publisher Malcom Forbes to participate in an early contest. Among the vehicles in Forbes' entourage was a Mercedes van, a vehicle previously unknown in the Helen area.

Pete and his ground crew ready the "Spirit of Helen" for flight.

9

Pete's willingness to face financial perils was matched by his desire to face physical danger as well. An automobile accident left him with a teflon plate to replace part of his skull; close scrapes in airplanes and his balloon added to his reputation for, as Mike Wilkins put it, "defying death in about every way possible". As the date for the 1976 race approached, stormy weather kept most balloonists on the ground.

Pete grew impatient, for the race was not living up to his promotional expectations. On a tempestuous day when the skies were filled with menacing thunderheads and everyone knew he shouldn't have flown, Pete lit the burners on his balloon, the "Spirit of Helen". Less than an hour later, the punctured craft was draped over high-tension power lines near Toccoa 30 miles to the east, its dauntless flyer lying lifeless on the ground below.

With Pete's death, the early period of Alpine development was over. The golf course was never completed. A windstorm toppled the bare block walls of the unfinished theater, which never rose from the rubble. The lone trolley car of the Helen Transit Authority today sits in the parking lot of the Alpenhof Motel, as if still waiting for its rails to arrive.

In the words of writer Phil Garner, Pete "flew as he lived, savoring the hazards".

However, although Helen lacked a central figure and things would take a different course, Alpine Helen was by then well established. Development continued in a more traditional and diffuse fashion as individual entrepreneurs and civic leaders made the investments and decisions which have shaped the town in the years since. Latter-day tourists now find several thousand rooms in the greater Helen area. Motels, shops and restaurants stretch up and down the three miles of the Helen valley. The Alpine Village does have a trolley, albeit one with rubber tires which roams about town offering rides to tourists after they have found a place to park. And Helen finally got a golf course, the Innsbruck Golf Resort located in an adjoining valley at the lower end of town. Several franchises have come to the Alpine Village, but McDonalds declined when refused an exemption from the Alpine theme which is still required in the central business district.

In the center of town, the city acquired a large hill where Helen's first tourist venture had been: it was the site of the Mountain Ranch Hotel, an upscale resort which displaced a pioneer cabin to stand there from the founding of Helen until being destroyed by a huge fire in 1945. Kudzu then claimed the site for nearly thirty years, but now it's a grassy expanse and arguably the prettiest spot in Helen.

With a walking trail and an array of benches and picnic tables, the hill is a fine place to relax and enjoy a good view of the forests which yet cloak the surrounding ridges, and to gaze down upon the mixture of Alpine and older, traditional architecture which comprises modern Helen. The grassy hilltop has an official name: it's known as "Pete's Park". The park was dedicated in memory of a free spirit, and perhaps also it's a fitting place to ponder things as they once were, as they might have been, and as they may turn out to be in this small stretch of valley on the headwaters of the Chattahoochee River.

*Eric Cook sits upon **"The Spirit of Helen"**, the first and only car of the "Helen Transit Authority" envisioned by Pete. The name was a joke, a play on Atlanta's new "MARTA" system, but unlike MARTA it would have been privately run.*

A CASE OF ALPINE EVOLUTION. The original conversion of Warren Brown's Station was faithful to John Kollock's rendering. Later, even trashcans were decorated in Alpine motif, although the tire-changer retained its original character.

Although Warren's original store had long since closed, he still owned the building 30 years after the Alpine conversion. With additions, it was home to seven Alpine shops, including Fantasy Lane *as shown in the painting by Donna Myers.*

WHEN HOLLYWOOD CAME CALLING.
In 1950, Susan Heyward, Rory Calhoun and other Hollwood notables came to film "I'd Climb the Highest Mountain". *Many locals appeared as extras. The scene where a young boy drowned was shot at Nora Mills; the funeral was filmed at* **Chattahoochee Methodist Church** *in Robertstown as depicted in the painting by folk artist Ken Woodall. The earliest movie known to have been made in the county was* "The Feud Girl", *an effort by New Yorkers filmed in the spring of 1916 and in theaters by the end of July when a special standing-room-only train carried White Countians to the Alamo Theater in Gainesville. In 1974, Burt Reynolds arrived in Helen via helicopter to film scenes for a* "Smoky and the Bandit" *movie. In the fall of 1997, Patrick Swayze and a Hollywood crew stayed in Helen while filming* "Black Dog".

CHAPTER 2: THEREABOUTS

*B*EFORE FOCUSING ON THE HELEN VALLEY, it's helpful to take a quick look around. At an elevation of about 1600 feet, Helen is 600 feet higher than Atlanta. The ridges on either side extend for over ten miles to the crest of the BLUE RIDGE as they climb to heights of nearly 4000 feet. Helen is on the headwaters of the Chattahoochee River, about 14 river miles below its high mountain source. Narrows at each end separate Helen from the Robertstown community above and the valley of Nacoochee below. Helen was not founded until a great sawmill was built there in 1912-13. Since the name was not previously applied to anything local, references to the "Helen valley" prior to 1913 are made only to locate the modern reader.

ROBERTSTOWN

*T*he neighboring community of Robertstown lies just a mile above Helen. In fact, it's so close that the operators of the Gainesville and Northwestern Railroad listed the station there as "North Helen", a designation never acceptable to a true Robertstown resident. The objection is justified, for Robertstown was a named community for years before Helen was created.

When the original Georgia surveyor came by in 1820, a man named Smith appears to have lived there, for his name was applied to the large tributary stream which joins the Chattahoochee River at Robertstown. However, this squatter did not remain.

ROBERTSTOWN. *Coming from the head of the River and bound for Helen, an early log train steams past Robertstown.*

The "first family" of Robertstown was that of John Trammell, who migrated from North Carolina and began purchasing land along the River and Smith Creek in 1821. Trammell eventually owned over 1000 acres which included nearly two miles of the Chattahoochee. His wife was Mary Mercer Fain, a daughter of the Ebenezer Fain who is ancestor to the Fains in the area today.

John Trammell's public activities included serving in the Georgia General Assembly and donating land for the CHATTAHOOCHEE METHODIST CHURCH in 1860. Scenes from the movie, *"I'd Climb the Highest Mountain"* were filmed at this church in 1950. Trammell was a slave owner whose sons served in the Civil War. After the war, the newly freed slaves remained on the Trammell estate and took the name of their former owners. This name still survives in the neighboring BEAN CREEK COMMUNITY, a black settlement which eventually became home to the Trammells and other former slaves from Nacoochee and Sautee who remained in the area.

When the white Trammells vacated the site after the war, the lands changed hands several times before being acquired around 1890 by Charles Roberts, a young, well-to-do Englishman who moved there as family representative for the Nacoochee Hills Gold Mining Company. The innovative Roberts also established greenhouses and a winery. Although no one objected to Roberts' vineyards in the late 1800s, more recent attempts to locate a winery in the county caused a considerable outcry before squeaking by at the polls with a winning margin of only 1% in a 1996 referendum. Among his many endeavors, Roberts built a new turnpike to parallel the old Unicoi Turnpike to Hiawassee, which had been temporarily abandoned. This road is still basically in use today as the Forest Service road which leaves GA 75 a mile north of Robertstown and runs through Indian Grave Gap to re-enter 75 on the other side of the mountain near the intersection of 75 and GA 180.

Roberts built a store beside the river at the north end of today's community. In 1903, Roberts filed an application for a post office there; it would be the "Robertstown" office, so the modern name was already in use by this time. He hired managers to run the store; among them was Jesse Clark who later joined with his two brothers to acquire it. Comer Vandiver recalled trading at Clarks Store when there was so little money around that skins could be used to make purchases: "If you had a large skin and it was worth more than the goods you bought, you'd get a little skin back as change."

Namesake's Resting Place. *Located across the Chattahoochee River atop a hill overlooking Robertstown, the inscription reads, "To Charles Roberts. Born at Weedon Beck, Northhamptonshire England. Died at Atlanta (22 May 1907). Aged 44 years. At Rest."*

ROBERTS STORE in about 1914. The Chattahoochee Bridge is on the left; from here the old Unicoi Turnpike ran up to Unicoi Gap, passing the entrance to Robert's competing "Mountain Scenic" turnpike on the way. As first the railroad and then modern highways reached Robertstown, its commercial district migrated down the river. This store was located about a mile above the intersection of GA 75 and the GA 356 turnoff to Unicoi State Park.

Robertstown was once a city, incorporated in 1913 the same as Helen, but folks there soon decided municipal affairs weren't worth the trouble and the township was dissolved. Although Robertstown no longer has its own post office, school or water system as it did for years, it retains a strong sense of community and has so far resisted occasional overtures to join the upstart city of Helen. Charles Robert's home is still occupied (and private); it's the last house standing above Highway 356 as one leaves Robertstown on the way to Unicoi State Park.

Roberts-Kimsey House

JOHN MARTIN HOUSE/NORA MILLS. *John Martin was a Scotsman who came to Georgia in the 1870s by way of London, England. Although Martin came to mine gold, he wound up marrying a local girl (a daughter of pioneer John Conley in the Helen valley) and, unike most miners, becoming a permanent resident. Acquiring rights to 1000s of acres, Martin operated both the Hamby Mining Ditch and the Martin Mine, the largest vein working in the area. Pioneer settler Daniel Brown established the first mill at the site of Nora Mills in the mid-1820s. Conley descendants say Martin's father-in-law John Conley, a carpenter, helped build the current mill building. After future Georgia governor Dr. Lamartine Hardman acquired the facility in 1905, he named it "Nora Mills" in memory of a sister and added an electric generator which supplied power to the Nichols-Hardman estate and the Crescent Hill Baptist Church.*

NACOOCHEE

*F*rom the Helen perspective, the storied "Vale of Nacoochee" begins at NORA MILLS, the old grist-mill which sits between Highway 75 and the Chattahoochee just below town. A gazebo-adorned INDIAN MOUND sits at Nacoochee's upper end, one of four such ancient mounds in this large valley. At its lower end, Sautee Creek enters from the adjoining valley of the same name, briefly crossing Nacoochee to merge with the waters of the Chattahoochee.

From the Nacoochee perspective, Helen is a new-comer, and a sometimes bothersome one at that. As home to the first churches, school, stores, hotel, and post office in the area, Nacoochee was the center of local pioneer life. And the Valley has the historical markers to prove it, as anyone who starts at the Indian Mound and wanders along Highway 75 will discover (one of these markers contains inaccuracies regarding the arrival of the first settlers). The place was a little different from the start, for many of its early settlers trace back along a piedmont migration path rather than that of the Scotch-Irish/mountaineers more often associated with the Georgia mountains.

Nacoochee has always elicited a stream of effusive prose from enthusiastic tourists and verbose valley dwellers. One early resident was Dr. Matthew Stephenson, a learned man of considerable vision who nonetheless was known for exaggeration, often saying "millions" when those about him thought he should have said "thousands". In 1870, Dr. Stephenson reported Nacoochee to be a center of western civilization as yet untouched by the notions of Charles Darwin:

> *The valley of Nacoochee. . . is considered by all foreigners to be one of the most charming and lovely valleys in the world. It is in a high state of cultivation, and improved by elegant residences, orchards, vineyards; and many of the choicest works of art in statuary and sculpture are being introduced from Italy to add to its beauty. Its inhabitants are natives of Massachusetts, Indiana, Virginia, Georgia, the Carolinas, and some from beyond the seas. They are pious, intelligent, and hospitable, and have yet to learn the cursed influence of European modern philosophy.*

The comments about Italian imports are a reference to the NICHOLS-HARDMAN HOUSE and grounds, which were then under construction. Today this elegant house stands amid huge magnolias at the intersection of Highways 17 and 75 in the west end of Nacoochee Valley (it's sometimes referred to as "West End"). The home was built by Captain J.H. Nichols, a wealthy Confederate veteran who moved up from the middle-Georgia town of Milledgeville after the war. Nichols also built the gazebo atop the Nacoochee Mound and the nearby CRESCENT HILL CHURCH. Nichols acquired thousands of acres, including lands at ANNA RUBY FALLS, which he named for his only daughter.

NICHOLS-HARDMAN HOUSE

Until the 1900s, "Nacoochee" was often used to describe a larger area encompassing neighboring valleys and habitations between the Blue Ridge and YONAH MOUNTAIN, the rocky prominence which overlooks it from the southwest. This area included the vales of Dukes Creek and Sautee, and the Helen valley until it finally got a name of its own.

Nacoochee is a different place even today, home to an eclectic group who tend to eschew the heavy development which Helen has seen. An alternative crowd gathers at the SWEETWATER COFFEE HOUSE, where the motto is "Sleepless in Sautee". The OLD SAUTEE STORE houses both a replica of an old country store and one of the finest gift shops around. Just up the road (GA 255), in the historic NACOOCHEE SCHOOL building, the SAUTEE-NACOOCHEE COMMUNITY CENTER AND MUSEUM is host to a variety of programs, including plays, art shows and a public museum displaying a growing collection of Indian, pioneer, and Gold Rush artifacts. For those still curious about the Valley, the museum offers copies of "NACOOCHEE -- ITS TIMES AND PLACES", a concise yet detailed guide to nearby historical sites by native-son Dr. Tom Lumsden.

CRESCENT HILL CHURCH. *Capt. J.H. Nichols had this church built in 1871. Nichols was a Presbyterian in a land of Methodists and Baptists; it housed a small Presbyterian congregation until 1898. After another two decades of intermittent use the Presbyterians returned the facility to Capt. Nichols only child Anna Ruby (Payne) in 1920. The following year Dr. Lamartine Hardman purchased the property from Anna Ruby and the church became home to the Baptists who continue there today. The church's story is told and illustrated in detail by Garrison Baker in* A History of Crescent Hill Church, *available in selected local shops and bookstores.*

THE CHATTAHOOCHEE

*I*t's often said locally that "Chattahoochee" originated with the Cherokees, but in fact the name was first applied far downstream in the territory of the Creek Indians. According to unpublished notes made by U.S. Indian Agent Benjamin Hawkins in 1798, the name was taken from the oldest Creek town on the river, "Chatto ho chee", a village which was probably located in Georgia's Heard County not too far from the Alabama line. As the name won acceptance among the whites, it steadily moved upstream, accompanied by a variety of spellings along the way.

However, for as long as the Cherokees remained on the Chattahoochee headwaters, the name only made it up to the edge of their territory. From the Cherokee perspective, the head of the river was known as "Chota River" or "Chota Creek", taken from their town of that name located at the gazebo-adorned NACOOCHEE MOUND.

With the departure of the Cherokees from the Nacoochee area, the memory of Chota quickly faded away. Map-makers eventually traced the river to its source, bestowing the title upon a small spring which lies a short distance below the crest of the Blue Ridge. The little spring was on Cherokee soil until the natives were finally forced from their last lands in 1838, and has been in Union County ever since. It's on the very edge of Union, though, running only a short distance before entering White County.

WHITE COUNTY AND CLEVELAND

W hite County was part of neighboring Habersham County until 1857, when it was carved out during the movement to create smaller counties. About a fourth of its 125,000 acres are owned by the government; most is Forest Service land in the mountains. Although there are many named communities, Helen and Cleveland are the only municipalities. Travelers entering the county via I-985 and GA 384/Duncan Bridge Road will pass GOURDCRAFT ORIGINALS,

WHITE COUNTY COURTHOUSE

which offers a free gourd museum along with hand-made gourd and other craft items in a pastoral setting with a lake and walking trail at the base of Mt. Yonah. To reach Gourdcraft from Helen, take GA 75 about 3 miles towards Cleveland and turn south (the only turn possible) on GA 384 for 2.3 miles.

The county seat has always been in the same location, but the town there was originally referred to as "Mt. Yonah" in reference to the nearby peak of the same name. The town was renamed for Benjamin Cleveland, a prominent northeast Georgian who distinguished himself in military affairs, business and politics in over half a century of service beginning in the early 1800s. The courthouse on the square was built by slaves out of hand-made bricks. Today the old building is home to the WHITE COUNTY HISTORICAL SOCIETY MUSEUM (tours free, donations accepted), which is open to visitors from Wednesday to Saturday.

Like Helen, downtown Cleveland found itself in a state of decline in the 1960s as local shoppers roared off towards Gainesville and Atlanta. After witnessing Helen's success as an Alpine village, Cleveland for a time considered remodeling itself as "Colonial Cleveland". Although some moves were made to dress up shops on the square, the idea never caught on. Time fixes some things, though, and modern Cleveland has gotten considerably busier as new stores and restaurants -- most of them off the square -- do quite well. Unfortunately, many older, locally owned businesses got displaced in the process.

However, the most prominent newer operation is home-grown: BABYLAND GENERAL HOSPITAL, home of the Cabbage Patch dolls, is the enterprise of White County native Xavier Roberts. During the height of the Cabbage Patch craze in 1983, many flocked to Cleveland to get original hand-made dolls; a few resourceful buyers even made random long-distance calls to Cleveland residents and hired them to stand in line at Babyland.

Babyland General is located just off Main Street one block south of the Cleveland square, where a huge stork holds a pointing sign. Colorful free tours feature "births" and end in the gift shop where locally handmade "babies" (the word "doll" is prohibited at Babyland) and the Mattel mass-produced versions are available for adoption (use of the word "purchase" is discouraged, although credit cards may be used to facilitate the arrangement).

BABYLAND GENERAL HOSPITAL

OVER-MOUNTAIN NEIGHBORS: FROM BLAIRSVILLE TO HIAWASSEE

State Highways 129, 75 and the Richard Russell Scenic Highway (GA 348) cross the Appalachian Trail on their way to the over-mountain counties of Union and Towns, which adjoin White County near the crest of the Blue Ridge. GA 180, the road leading to BRASSTOWN BALD (Georgia's highest peak), connects to all of these highways. Following one of these routes across the mountain and returning by another offers a good day-trip from the Helen area. Although only one is now designated a "scenic highway", all offer spectacular mountain vistas and access to trails and recreation areas.

BLAIRSVILLE is the Union County seat. US 129 from Cleveland to Blairsville was the first local automobile road constructed across the Blue Ridge. At the top of the mountain, NEELS GAP was renamed for the state highway engineer who oversaw the work; the WALASI-YI CENTER there retains the original Cherokee name for the locale and offers mountain art, books, outdoor gear, and refreshments to travelers. The APPALACHIAN TRAIL passes through the interesting stone building which houses the center.

Union County is also home to VOGEL STATE PARK, one of the state's oldest and prettiest, which stands below looming visage of BLOOD MOUN-TAIN. In addition to camping (always full on summer and fall weekends), Vogel offers swimming, rental cabins (call months in advance), access to many hiking trails and even miniature golf, an odd activity for a state park.

The Towns County seat is HIAWASSEE, a growing retirement mecca which stands beside scenic Lake Chatuge under the watchful gaze of Brasstown Bald and is home to the annual GEORGIA MOUNTAIN FAIR. Many have profited as the place has boomed, but not everyone has enjoyed watching as cabins climb the surrounding hills to appropriate once pristine views. A little further west, the town of YOUNG HARRIS sports YOUNG HARRIS COL-LEGE and BRASSTOWN VALLEY RESORT, a project supported by Demo-cratic Governor Zell Miller and said to have therefore been "the only golf course ever opposed by Republicans". In addition to golf, Brasstown Valley offers a spectacular lodge and highly rated restaurant.

LOCATION OF THE CENTER OF THE EARTH

While it may not be quite the "center of the earth" as Pete Hodkinson put it (a premise never accepted by Robertstown or Nacoochee and certainly not Cleveland), Helen is located in the northeast corner of Georgia. As the crow flies, North and South Carolina are less than 25 miles away and the Tennessee state line only about 40 miles distant. But since crows have a considerable advantage in the north Georgia mountains, the distances by automobile are nearly twice as far.

Until the Civil War, northeast Georgia looked eastward towards Charleston, Augusta and Savannah for economic and political affairs. After the War, the focus turned to the west and the city of Atlanta, which at the time was a compact town 90 miles from the Helen valley. In recent years metro Atlanta has raced northward at a rapid pace to occupy about half of the countryside which once separated the two, a northward march which will accelerate if Atlanta's proposed Outer Perimeter and the so-called "Foothills Scenic Parkway" (actually a commercial road mainly intended to "straighten the curves" from Dalton to Toccoa) are ever constructed.

But with Helen's rise as a tourist town, it's probably a safe guess that at least half of Atlanta comes anyway to visit during the summer and fall seasons. Visitors have always come to the mountains, though, even without the ease of modern transportation or the inducements of Helen's contemporary Alpine commerce. In fact, the first tourists weren't all that far behind the first settlers. There's just something special about the mountains, a sentiment well expressed by Dr. Stephenson in the flush prose of an earlier era:

> *From the trending of the mountains the upheaved strata form thousands of waterfalls. . . in addition to which the charming landscapes, the magnificent scenery, and the sublime accompaniments of mountain grandeur, elevate the mind and fill the soul with the most exquisite and indescribable emotions, bringing man into close communion with his Creator and Preserver.*

Amen, and may it ever be so!

CHICKAMAUGA CREEK COVERED BRIDGE. *After years of splashing across or being forced to wait until flood waters receded, wooden bridges eventually offered relief from troublesome fords on larger streams. Most remained in service until replaced by modern structures, but the bridge across the Chattahoochee at Robertstown was collapsed in 1929 when Paul Westmoreland Sr. attempted to drive the county's new 10-ton tractor across. Paul, the tractor and the bridge all went into the river. The last of the old bridges is this covered span in Sautee Valley, located about two miles from the Old Sautee Store on GA 255. Today the Highway Department maintains the site as a park. In the mid-1950s picture taken when the bridge was still in use, barefooted Joyce and Tommy Tallant are set against a backdrop of haystacks.*

CHAPTER 3: EARLY HISTORY

INDIAN TIMES AND TALES

THE CENTER OF LOCAL INDIAN AFFAIRS was Nacoochee Valley. Modern archaeologists have determined the area was occupied for thousands of years by cultures which preceded the known tribes; the four ancient ceremonial mounds in Nacoochee are a legacy of these vanished peoples. Such mounds were mysterious even to the Cherokees, who told early explorers they did not build them and didn't know who did.

Working with meager clues from their excavations, researchers have done an amazing job of determining time-lines and reconstructing life-styles of the hunter-gatherers and primitive farmers who long ago occupied the wild expanses of America. Even so, we know little of the rites and rituals which sustained them or the feel of the times in which they lived.

In contrast, since Europeans appeared and began writing things down, much more is known about the Cherokees. Their first recorded visitors were Spaniards who came from the south looking for gold. Although the Spanish did not colonize the Cherokee country, they did leave a lasting legacy: they called the Southern mountains the "Appalachians" since they had been sent in that direction by the Appalachee Indians in Florida.

As these projectile points attest, *Native Americans occupied Nacoochee and surrounding areas for thousands of years before the settlers came. Many Indian, pioneer and Gold Rush artifacts are on display at the Sautee-Nacoochee Community Association Museum.*

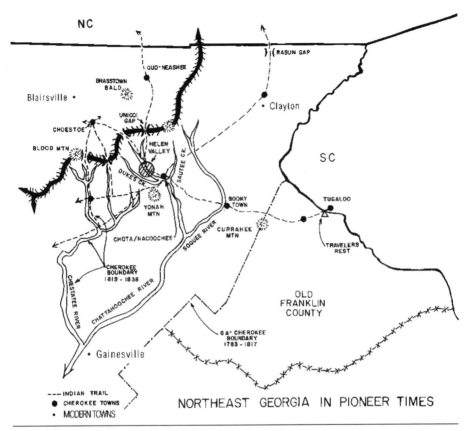

NC

QUO-NEASHEE

RABUN GAP

BRASSTOWN
BALD

Blairsville •

UNICOI
GAP

• Clayton

CHOESTOE

BLOOD MTN

HELEN
VALLEY

SC

DUKES CK

SAUTEE CK.

YONAH
MTN

SOOKY
TOWN

TUGALOO

CHOTA/NACOOCHEE

SOQUEE RIVER

CURRAHEE
MTN

TRAVELERS
REST

CHEROKEE
BOUNDARY
1819 - 1838

CHESTATEE RIVER

CHATTAHOOCHEE RIVER

OLD
FRANKLIN
COUNTY

GA - CHEROKEE
BOUNDARY
1783 - 1817

• Gainesville

--- INDIAN TRAIL
● CHEROKEE TOWNS
• MODERN TOWNS

NORTHEAST GEORGIA IN PIONEER TIMES

In the 1800s it was widely believed that Spanish explorer Desoto had visited Nacoochee, but later studies led scholars to conclude his expedition went east and north of the area. However, since other Spaniards also travelled through the region and the possibility of their presence cannot be entirely discounted, tales connecting the Spanish to lost mines and mysterious buried habitations will probably always be told on the Chattahoochee headwaters.

The first white men known for sure to have visited the Helen/Nacoochee area were Englishmen who came from the South Carolina Colony around 1700. The earliest written accounts describe visits to the local villages of Nacoochee and Chota in 1715 and again in 1725. Chota was located beside the gazebo-adorned Indian Mound at the upper end of Nacoochee Valley. Unfortunately for the Chotas, after the Cherokees sided with the British during the Revolution, their town was also visited at least twice by American militiamen. The soldiers reported many houses and great fields of corn, all of which they destroyed.

At the close of the Revolution the Indian boundary in Georgia was fixed about 30 miles southeast of Helen, where it remained for 40 years. Georgians officially referred to this line as the "Western Frontier". In the Helen/Nacoochee area, during this period between the Revolution and the coming of the settlers, the town of Chota was abandoned and the nearby village of Nacoochee was described as a town "where fully half of its inhabitants were half-breeds said to be a mixture of Cherokee Indian and Torys of the Revolution".

In 1819, a treaty with the Cherokees put the Helen/Nacoochee area on Georgia soil about 10 miles outside the Indian boundary. But for nearly twenty years after the first settlers arrived, the Cherokees were not too far away, the closest residing about 15 miles north just across the Blue Ridge and others about 20 miles to the west across the Chestatee River.

During this time, they made occasional visits to their former territory. On Dukes Creek, Mrs. John Richardson was surprised by a group of Cherokees who suddenly appeared in her yard while her husband, a travelling Methodist minister, was off riding his circuit. Although such encounters were unsettling given the legacy of violence along the frontier, she bravely bade them to spend the night at her place. They accepted, sleeping outside, and had quietly melted again into the woods by the time she arose the next morning.

RICHARDSON-LUMSDEN HOUSE. Built in 1830 with sawn boards from a water-driven "sash" sawmill on nearby Dukes Creek, this was the home of pioneer settler John Richardson, a circuit-riding Methodist minister.

Although the Cherokees across the Blue Ridge and the Chestatee were finally rounded up and sent westward on the Trail of Tears in 1838, Indians remained objects of great curiosity, as they do even today. And since human nature is like Mother Nature in that it abhors a vacuum, the more fanciful of the new white residents on the old Cherokee lands created a series of tales to satisfy inquisitive local minds.

One thing these stories show is how little the settlers knew about their Indian predecessors. Many local tales were either created or amplified by George Williams, who came to Nacoochee as a pioneer child and went off to Charleston to become one of the wealthiest merchants in the South before returning to improve upon the history of the area in dramatic fashion.

Perhaps the best known of the Indian tales concerns the gazebo-adorned Nacoochee Mound, supposedly raised by the Cherokees as the final resting place of the lovely princess Nacoochee and her noble lover Sautee, who was from a different tribe (usually said to be Chickasaw) and fell in love with the beautiful maiden as his party passed through the valley. Nacoochee was likewise smitten, but since marriage between tribes was forbidden, running off was the only option.

After a search by her father's warriors, the unlucky lovers were found atop nearby Mount Yonah, whereupon Sautee was promptly flung from high cliffs there. The distraught Nacoochee then threw herself over the precipice to conclude a tragic tale suspiciously reminiscent of one already told by Shakespeare, and in more modern times, a host of offerings from the entertainment industry, including the 1960s ballad "Running Bear" by country singer Sonny James, which is a near-perfect match for the Nacoochee story.

But even if the concept of a "princess" was alien to the Cherokees and the mound had been built well before they arrived, bothering with such details would only have hindered a good tale which conveniently explained the origin of two local placenames. Taking things a little further, George Williams claimed that "Nacoochee" meant "evening star" in Cherokee, a fanciful notion since the word has no meaning in that language and in fact appears to have originated with the Creek Indians and thus be one of the many indications that they occupied the area before being evicted by the Cherokees.

In florid style, Williams also concocted detailed accounts of the battles, romances and intrigue which occurred during Desoto's mythical visit. Interest-

Mt. Yonah Looms Over the Nacoochee Mound.

ingly, Williams had some exposure to factual accounts of Desoto's expedition, for he used the names of actual expedition members in his wild narratives. Other local Indian tales concern lost Indian treasure caves and gold mines, even though there is virtually no evidence that the Cherokees mined or even had much interest in the precious metal when they occupied the Helen/Nacoochee area.

Part of the fun of these myths, though, is that they have long since taken on a life of their own and people are still adding to them. In recent years, one man claimed to have been taken to a treasure cave on Mt. Yonah as a little boy, but since he was so young, he couldn't remember how to get back. Some who have climbed on the cliffs of Mt. Yonah have found a spot where the rock is stained a dark color, and of course this must be the very spot where the bodies of Sautee and Nacoochee splattered against the face of the cliff.

And down where the valleys of Nacoochee and Sautee come together, a latter day resident allowed as how he had determined that an ancient oak, which happened to be right beside his store, was the very tree under which the ill-fated Indian lovers had met. He put up a sign to tell the tale, and for years relayed the story with a sparkle in his eye and what appeared to be the edges of a mostly-hidden smile teasing the corners of his mouth.

OLD SAUTEE STORE. *Adding a twist to the myth of Sautee and Nacoochee, the aged oak tree whose limb appears to the far right was said to have been 400 years old and witness to the ill-fated lovers' first meeting. Appropriately enough, in the mid-1990s the tree was destroyed by a bolt of lightning. This building housed the Nacochee Post Office from 1873 until the early 1960s; after it closed, Mervin and Astrid Fried turned the "Old Sautee Store" into one of the most-visited attractions in the area.*

THE NACOOCHEE TOTEM POLE *was carved by George Eastman, a talented itinerant artist who came to spend his last years in Nacoochee. Although people persist in erecting totem poles and tepees across north Georgia, neither of these Hollywood symbols were ever associated with the Cherokees, whose houses typically had walls of dried mud and sticks until they acquired iron tools from the white man and began building log cabins. Mr. Eastman is nonetheless recognized for his artistry: samples of his work -- including a section of the totem pole -- can be seen at the Sautee-Nacoochee Community Association Museum.*

OLD CHOTA. *Near the intersection of GA 17/75, the gazebo-adorned Indian mound stands at Nacoochee Valley's upper end, overlooking the former site of the Cherokee village of Chota (also called "Little Chota" in deference to their capitol of the same name located on the Little Tennessee River). The roofs of Alpine Helen appear in the middle of the picture; the old Unicoi Turnpike ran through the Helen valley on its way to cross the Blue Ridge at Unicoi Gap. For nearly 20 years after the first settlers came, until the Removal and the Trail of Tears in 1838, the lands across the Blue Ridge were the domain of the Cherokees.*

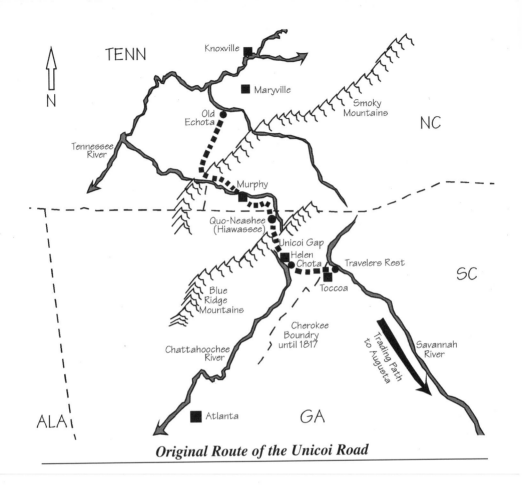

Original Route of the Unicoi Road

THE UNICOI ROAD

ALTHOUGH IT'S HARD TO IMAGINE TODAY, Helen's Main Street follows the route of an ancient trail, a major Southeastern trading route on the network of footpaths which criss-crossed the American wilderness for thousands of years before Europeans arrived. The old trail forded the Chattahoochee twice on its way through the Helen valley; once where the Main Street bridge is and again just above the Hoffbrau Haus at the north end of town.

In 1813, a treaty was negotiated for the improvement of the trail into a wagon road by the Unicoi Turnpike Company, which was to pay the Cherokees $160 per year for the privilege of operating it as a toll road through their nation. The route began on the Tugaloo River east of Toccoa, at the head of navigation on the Savannah River system. In this area, the road also crossed another wagon route leading down the west bank of the Savannah River to Augusta and the coast.

OLD AND NEW ON THE UNICOI ROAD. *This 1930s picture was taken at the upper end of Helen, just upstream and across the River from today's Hoffbrau Haus. On the old Unicoi Road, where it once forded the River, Henry Abernathy stands behind the little wagon carrying Anna and Leigh Gedney. In the background, the present Highway 75 to Roberstown is under construction.*

Construction with hand tools and animal-power through the rugged mountains of Georgia, North Carolina and Tennessee took longer than expected, but by 1819 the Unicoi Road was finished all the way to its terminus near present day Maryville, Tennessee, to become "the great highway from the coast to the Tennessee settlements". Drovers with herds of horses, cattle and even flocks of turkeys joined the purveyors of furs and leather in a southward procession, bound for markets at Augusta, Savannah, and Charleston. Wagons loaded with manufactured goods and necessary supplies rolled back to the frontier regions.

Roadhouses were constructed at 20 mile intervals along the turnpike; one was located in Nacoochee Valley to offer weary travellers warm fires, cooked meals, hot coffee and dry beds, even if it might be necessary to share one with a stranger. Outside, food was available for the stock; drovers would sometimes leave part of their herd as payment for the hospitality they received.

The Unicoi Turnpike was over 150 miles long in its early days, but as lands were acquired from the Cherokees, the parts in settled areas became public roads. By the Civil War, the remaining Georgia section operated as a private road was the rugged, six-mile stretch which crossed the Blue Ridge at Unicoi Gap about 10 miles above Helen. After a break in service, this portion was again gated and operated as a toll road until the mid-1920s.

Until the 1930s, the route of the Unicoi Road through Helen and Nacoochee was basically unchanged, except that bridges replaced the worst of the old fords which travelers had splashed across for centuries. When the State Highway Department arrived in the late 1930s with convict labor, bulldozers and powerful explosives, they bypassed the old ford at the Hoffbrau Haus, choosing instead to apply their new technology in blasting a new route along the east side of the River to Robertstown.

Above Robertstown, the new State Road 75 rejoined the old Unicoi route for several miles before the engineers again departed below Andrews Cove to carve a more gradual route on up the mountainside to UNICOI GAP, leaving sections of the meandering old turnpike to be reclaimed at last by the Appalachian woods. Visitors parking at UNICOI GAP can easily find the old road by walking into the valleys on either side.

PIONEER DAYS

ONCE THE CHEROKEES WERE GONE, the story of the Helen valley of course becomes a story of the American frontier. Georgia surveyors were at work only a few months after the Cherokee treaty of 1819 transferred the headwaters of the Chattahoochee to the State. The Helen/Nacoochee area was divided into 250 acre "Land Lots" and distributed to male Georgia citizens (or their widows or orphans) and certain U.S. veterans in the 1820 Land Lottery. However, few of the lucky lottery winners ever moved to their new property.

Instead, the Chattahoochee headwaters were settled by two groups of pioneers who had begun their frontier migrations far to the north well over a century before. Those of the piedmont culture came with money and slaves to manage large farms in the fertile bottom areas along the river. In the smaller valleys on the tributaries and back in the mountain coves, those of more limited means established family farms in the mountaineer tradition. To a noticeable extent, descendants of these groups occupy the same areas today.

These settlers came to a land where the narrow paths of Indians disappeared into a great wilderness still echoing with the cries of wolves and panthers. The first landowner in the Helen valley was Elijah England, who bought his 250 acres from the lottery winner for $1000 in 1822. However, in restless frontier fashion, Elijah and several other early residents stayed for only a few years before picking up to move yet again as new lands opened to the west.

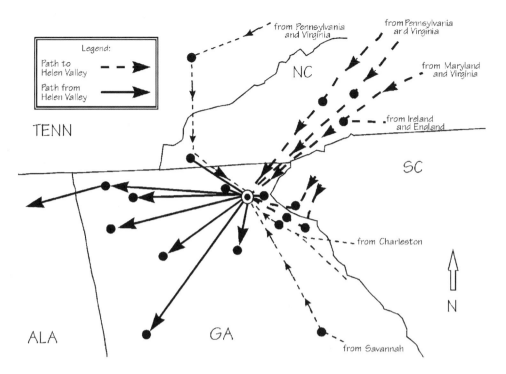

MIGRATION PATHS. *The Helen area was opened for settlement in 1820. Most settlers came from two areas: the first came from the nearby Georgia counties of Habersham and Franklin; pioneers from the North Carolina foothills started arriving soon after. Some early arrivals came from other areas such as middle Georgia, South Carolina, and down the Unicoi Road from the backwoods settlements in Tennessee. Migrants came from both the piedmont and mountaineer migrations which had originated in Pennsylvania, Virginia and Maryland and which were joined by immigrants arriving at more southern ports as they pushed south and west. The frontier was delayed in the Helen valley for over a decade by the Cherokees. When it opened again, many valley pioneers picked up and followed it westward, as did many of the children of permanent settlers who remained in the area.*

It took a while for things to calm down, but by the early 1830s, four pioneer families had settled in to make the Helen valley a more permanent home. At the upper end of the valley, the family of Richard and Patsy England occupied the fields above the Alpine Crest resort. The Henry Highland Conley clan built a house atop the hill in the middle of town where Pete's Park is now located. At the lower end of the valley, Montgomery and Comfort Bell worked their fields where the Loreli time-sharing resort now stands. Across the river from the Bells, Adam and Rachel Pitner lived along the small creek which passes beside the Alpine Amusement Park. The Englands and Conleys also had slaves who lived in separate houses.

The valley was a busy place as the newcomers worked to build their cabins and farms. Split-rail fences and small outbuildings appeared in the spreading fields while a parade of strangers passed by on the Unicoi Road. The pioneer families grew also, as over 40 youngsters ran along the banks of the Chattahoochee in the 1830s, more than live there today. These largely self-sufficient farmers made their own cloth and leather. A blacksmith lived on the Pitner Place and corn was ground at a nearby grist-mill.

Valley residents served the Southern cause in the Civil War; Coleman England came home to die and was buried in the old England Cemetery at the lower end of the valley. When the War was over, the newly-freed slaves left to start new lives elsewhere. John Conley, the last of the original pioneers to live in the valley, died in 1890. Other mountaineers came to take their place, though, leaving the affairs of living largely unchanged until 1913, when the Gainesville and Northwestern Railroad steamed into the valley and the new town of Helen was established.

PIONEER CHILDREN. *Moving on in the frontier direction, several children of pioneer settler Richard England migrated over the Blue Ridge to Union County in the 1830s and 40s. This couple is said to be second-son Daniel England and his apparently-pregnant wife, circa 1850. Their log house still stands beside GA 129 just north of the intersection with GA 180.*

GOLD RUSH DAYS

*T*HERE ARE RIVAL CLAIMS about when and where Georgia gold was discovered. Several accounts place the find about thirty miles southwest of Helen in various locations near Dahlonega. The local claim is that gold was first discovered on Dukes Creek, a Chattahoochee tributary three miles west of Helen. This assertion was always supported by Dr. Matthew Stephenson, one of the most colorful figures of the Georgia Gold Rush and long-time resident of both areas, who said the find was on Dukes Creek in 1828.

OLD ENGLAND VEIN, photographed in about 1895. Today, this site is open as "The Gold Mines of Helen".

In any event, the Gold Rush was certainly in full swing by 1830 as land prices skyrocketed and thousands of gold-seekers swarmed over the region. Using primarily gold pans and sluice boxes, the first miners worked rich stream-side deposits where gold had been concentrated by countless millennia of erosive action. Although there was some work on the hillsides and hard-rock veins, early miners largely stayed near the creeks since water was available to "wash" their sandy ore and separate the heavy gold from lighter materials.

In 1830, John Humphries appeared on the Richard England Place at the lower end of the Helen valley. After finding gold beside the river there, Humphries and other investors struck a deal to buy half of Richard's lands, where operations were soon underway at the "England Mine". The Englands eventually collected about $17,000 from Humphries and company, less than they were promised but still a very substantial sum for mountain farmers who had acquired the land for about $750 only a few years before.

In a story repeated many times across the Georgia gold region, things didn't go so well for Humphries and company. After early success finding gold in the sands beside the river, they lost their investments and more when they tried burrowing into the hard bedrock beside the Chattahoochee River. They were the first in a series of operators who had the same dismal experience over the next 60 years. Today, the England Mine is more successful: the site is a tourist attraction open to visitors as "The Gold Mines of Helen".

Although the initial fervor of the Gold Rush abated before 1840, significant mining operations continued in the Helen area until World War II. If the Rush was gone, occasional cases of gold fever were not. Over the next century, a series of outsiders came through, often paying outrageously high prices for old mines. While most came away poorer for the experience, there were winners in the local gold fields.

The pioneer valley residents did not succumb to gold fever, but they didn't have to. They already owned lands where gold was found, which they worked with some success. They didn't strike it rich, but one man who came later to the Helen valley did make substantial sums on his gold operations.

J.R. Dean was a New England school teacher who moved South in the 1850s, seeking a gentler climate when his health declined. Travelling down the Unicoi Road, as he approached the Helen valley the mule he was riding tired of the many stream crossings on the way down from Unicoi Gap. When the balky animal finally refused to go any further, J.R. struck up a conversation with a passing mountaineer who told him there was money to be made mining gold.

J.R. DEAN FAMILY. A native New-Englander and former school teacher who became a gold-miner extraordinaire, J.R. Dean was about 50 years old when this picture was taken. From the left, family members are Herbert Henry, Clara, Mary and wife Rebecca Cook Dean. After acquiring the lands of pioneer settler Richard England, the Deans built a home across the river from today's Hoffbrau Haus and just above the former site of Orbit Manufacturing Company.

Over the next quarter of a century, this transplanted New Englander and accidental valley resident became the most successful of all the miners who labored there. Realizing water was the key to profitable mining, J.R. built great mining ditches to transport the waters of local creeks to areas beyond the reach of earlier miners. The simplest of these canals ran along the foot of the mountains, re-routing creeks to reach untouched gold deposits on the valley floors.

In more dramatic fashion, J.R. built a high ditch to capture the waters of Dukes Creek just below Dukes Creek Falls. Today, these falls are reached by travelling the Richard Russell Scenic Highway and hiking down a one-mile trail. From the falls, the "Hamby Ditch" ran nearly level along the mountainside for eight miles before crossing the Hamby Mountain ridge through Whitehorse Gap to reach the Helen valley and the lands of J.R. Dean. At this point, the borrowed waters of Dukes Creek were over 200 feet above the valley floor.

Water from the ditch was then run down the mountain in iron pipes to build tremendous pressure before being directed through the tapering nozzles of "water cannons". The resulting powerful streams of water sliced through the virgin Georgia soil with "magical rapidity", sending torrents of soil and rock down the slopes to be milled and sluiced below. Known as "hydraulic mining", this process left parts of the gold region so barren that early film makers came to the Georgia hills to use them as back-drops for western movies.

GOLDEN EGG. W. G. Hudson holds a 5 and 1/2 ounce gold nugget found on Dukes Creek in May, 1936. The nugget is rounded and stream-worn, indicating it has been transported for some distance from the source vein. After restoring the Hamby Ditch for its final years of use before World War II, Hudson found a considerable amount of gold.

On the face of Hamby Mountain overlooking the Helen valley, J.R. worked for years to cut a huge gash which became known as the "Dean Cut", from which a State geologist noted "he is reported to have reaped a rich harvest". And when J.R. died in 1884 after nearly thirty years as a north Georgia gold miner, his estate was worth many times that of his mountain neighbors.

Except for the part-time labors of the locals, gold mining in the area had all but ceased by 1900. However, when the government raised the price of gold by 70% in 1933, there was one last burst of activity. Using technology unavailable to early miners, the Franco-American Mining Company spent a considerable sum drilling into the side of Hamby Mountain where J.R. Dean had successfully applied the waters of the Hamby Ditch 60 years before, but their operations were not profitable.

Ironically, while Franco-American's try at hard-rock mining failed, the old high ditch built by J.R Dean 80 years before was put back into operation with some success. Under W.G. Hudson, the Hamby Ditch was extended to new areas which yielded considerable amounts of gold until all mining activities were halted by executive order during World War II.

Since then, gold mining has mostly been the province of hobbyists and a few locals who still go at it part-time, or an off-shoot of sand and gravel operations which must dig anyway in the same deposits where gold has collected. However, for modern tourists working a pan-full of sandy "ore" at one of the local panning places or visiting the "Goldmines of Helen", it's still hard not to get a touch of gold fever. After all, there's still gold in "them thar' Georgia hills", where some big nuggets have yet to be found!

HAMBY MINING DITCH. The four illustrations on the following pages demonstrate the workings of the old mining ditches built along many streams in the Georgia gold region. After capturing a mountain stream on its headwaters, a ditch was run along the mountain-side with as little fall as possible. As it proceeded down the valley, the nearly-level ditch attained ever greater heights above the rapidly descending stream in the valley below. The first picture shows the intake for the Hamby Mining Ditch, located just below Dukes Creek Falls. From there, as detailed on the map, the nearly-level canal ran through earthen ditches and an occasional flume for 8 miles to reach the Helen valley, where its waters were over 200 feet above the valley floor. Using the hydraulic mining technique shown on the next page, J.R. Dean worked for years in the "Dean Cut", from which he was "reported to have reaped a rich harvest".

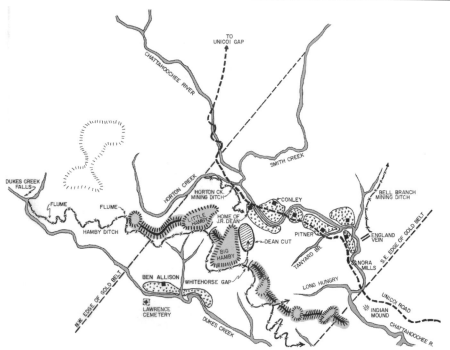

HYDRAULIC MINING. *Along the lower reaches of the Hamby Ditch, pipes were run down the mountain to build water pressure before being connected to "water cannons". The resulting powerful streams of water sliced into the Georgia hills with "magical rapidity", freeing tons of gold -bearing material to be washed and sluiced down below.*

CHAPTER 4: THE TWENTIETH CENTURY ARRIVES

IN THE LENGTHENING SHADOW OF THE FRONTIER

ALTHOUGH OUTSIDE FORCES were already moving to impose big changes, if any of the pioneer settlers of the Helen valley had somehow been able to visit there as 1911 began, they would have had little trouble recognizing the place. The fields they had begun to clear nearly a century before were still pretty much like they had left them, as were some of the log cabins they raised for shelter. The old Unicoi Road on which they had arrived was still the main thoroughfare, crossing the river twice to follow the same path as always.

With their modest needs, the residents of the upper Chattahoochee had only nibbled along the edges of the great virgin wood which still cloaked the surrounding mountains. Two early timbering operations likewise had little effect: a small, steam-driven sawmill operated for a time on the Tanyard Branch at the lower end of the Helen valley and, further up the river, a more ambitious attempt at "splash-dam" logging failed when the shallow Chattahoochee proved uncooperative in floating logs down-river to mills near Gainesville. These brief forays were precursors of what was to come.

In the lengthening shadow of the Georgia frontier, a handful of families lived and farmed in the same way as their predecessors had done, growing their own food, weaving cloth for the family clothes, and bartering for other necessities. A traveler coming into the upper end of the Helen valley on the old Unicoi Road would have first encountered Jesse Hicks, who resided in the former home of gold-miner J.R. Dean. This house, which later burned, was located just above the factory building which once housed Orbit Manufacturing Company.

After crossing the upper ford to continue down the road past the present day Hoffbrau Haus and Chattahoochee Motel, the traveler next would have encountered Dave and Alvena Fain, who were raising their family in a house near today's "Betty Fain's Country Store", or simply "Betty's" as it is locally known. It's not totally coincidental, of course, that Betty's is owned and operated by descendants of Dave and Alvena Fain, who returned in the 1970s to re-occupy the spot.

As the traveler passed the hill where Pete's Park now sits, he would have looked up to see an old log house where Lum Westmoreland lived with his wife of 44 years and their youngest daughter. Both Dave and Lum lived on lands first occupied by the pioneer Conleys, an area which they soon would leave as it became the site of the original downtown area of Helen.

After crossing the river ford where today's modern concrete bridge stands, the traveler would have next noted the home occupied by Elisha Wright, located below the Unicoi Road on the site now occupied by Wendy's restaurant and the White County Bank. Proceeding down the valley, John Robinson, Jim Wheeler and John Westmoreland are said to have lived on the upper side of the road.

When the Missourians arrived in 1911, they found a handful of families living in the Helen Valley, including the family of Dave and Alvena Fain, pictured here in their later years. When Helen was established, the Fains moved about a mile up the river to a terraced hill-side farm site still occupied by their descendants.

As the traveler approached the lower end of the Helen valley, he would find three families residing along the small creek known as the Tanyard Branch, above the present sites of the Alpine Amusement Park and Alpine Putt-Putt. Longest in residence there was George Slaton, who operated a store on a high bank close beside the Unicoi Road, so close that Fannie Vandiver Lusk remembers wondering why it didn't just tumble over into the road. Bob Logan, a blacksmith, lived near Mr. Slaton.

The Tanyard Branch was also home to G.A. and Lula Crumley Vandiver, who had recently migrated down to the Helen valley from their former home high on the headwaters of the Chattahoochee River. "Dandy" and "Lou", as they were known, remained on their land for the rest of their independent days, where 85 years later two of their children remained to head up members of four generations of descendants who still resided on the Tanyard Branch.

A TOWN IS BORN

Comer Vandiver, son of Dandy and Lou Vandiver, remembers the day in 1911 when several men arrived in a fancy chauffeured car. Comer and his brothers were working his father's fields in a place where very few automobiles had ever been seen; the residents there could remember every one. The passengers in the car were from St. Louis, Missouri, and they were interested in buying some of his father's land.

The events leading up to this visit had taken place over the previous decade, as speculators began buying up land and timber rights in the northeast Georgia mountains. During this period, a large tract on the headwaters of the Chattahoochee River was assembled by a wealthy businessman from Charleston, SC. In 1911, this tract was acquired by the Byrd-Matthews Lumber Company, a venture headed up by St. Louis businessmen Joseph R. Byrd and J.L. and Charles Matthews.

However, the first Missourian to do business in the Helen valley was John Mitchell. Although certainly associated with Byrd and Matthews, he acted on his own to buy considerable acreage in 1911 from Dandy Vandiver, Lum Westmoreland, and others so that he soon owned about half of the Helen valley and most of the land where **Robertstown** now sits. Although latter-day Helen leaders took pride in the speed with which Helen was converted into an Alpine village, the Bavarian conversion wasn't a whole lot faster than the creation of the town in the first place.

After selling Byrd-Matthews the site for their sawmill, Mitchell in less than two years fathered the new municipalities of Helen and **Robertstown**, where lots were being sold before 1912 was done. Overlooking the emerging city of Helen, he tore down the house where Lum Westmoreland had lived and began construction of "The Mitchell Mountain Ranch", a luxurious hotel which offered access to the first flush-toilets in a land of out-houses, and even had such contraptions on every floor. Dandy Vandiver started construction on Helen's first store building. Work was delayed only temporarily when a rare cyclone passed through, leveling both.

Across the river from the new Mountain Ranch Hotel, on the former homeplace last occupied by Elisha Wright, Byrd-Matthews moved with equal speed to build the huge sawmill which would process the harvest from their many thousands of acres of virgin timber. The mill was under construction by 1912 as the first parts began arriving by wagon. However, the Missourians plans did not rest upon the use of wagons.

MOUNTAIN RANCH. John Mitchell began construction of the 23-room "Mitchell Mountain Ranch" in 1912. After the property was acquired by Will and Charles White in 1921, they added 27 rooms, more indoor plumbing, and changed the name to the "Mountain Ranch Hotel". In its heyday, it was a popular summer resort; among the up-scale amenities offered were a nine-hole golf course, tennis and shuffleboard courts, a spring-fed swimming pool, horses and trails, and a large pavilion where both guests and locals enjoyed Wednesday and Saturday night dances. The hotel burned in 1945.

As Mitchell laid out his towns and work began on the sawmill, the ingredient which was key to their plans was also moving along at a rapid pace: the tracks of the Gainesville and Northwestern Railroad were progressing steadily along the 37 miles they had to cover to reach the stations at Helen and Robertstown.

When the first engines of the G.&.N.W.R.R. steamed into Helen early in 1913, activity increased. The last pieces of the mill came in on the train and by 1914, the mill was in full operation. Businesses and houses continued to be built on Mitchell's lots. The mill constructed a number of small, simple homes to house its laborers; larger and fancier homes were built for the managers. More hotels were constructed, including the Commercial Hotel downtown and the three-story Marshall Hotel which overlooked the sawmill. Helen soon had a drugstore, cafe, boarding-house, bank, barber shop, pool hall, and a post office. A doctor was in residence at the company medical clinic.

A NEW TOWN TAKES SHAPE. In this July, 1913 picture of Main Street, the original iron bridge across the Chattahoochee is already in place as work continues on the first downtown buildings. The bridge was second-hand when it came to town and has since been moved twice to its present location above Loreli time-sharing resort. Later Helenites were proud of the speed with which the Alpine conversion was accomplished, but it didn't take much longer to create the new town in the first place.

Several stores located in Helen. B.A. Rogers & Co. advertised itself as "Helen's Largest Store", offering everything from clothes to Christmas presents. Rogers also solicited "your Chickens, Eggs, Beans, Peas, etc." for which they claimed to pay the highest prices. At about the same time, Charlie Maloof purchased several downtown lots and relocated the Maloof Brothers Store from neighboring Cleveland.

The Maloof brothers had recently immigrated from Lebanon; Charlie always spoke with the noticeable accent of one who learns a second language later in life. Although the Helen site was acquired in the names of Charlie and his brother Solomon, only Charlie remained as "Sol" settled in Bryson City, NC. Charlie had already made forays into the Helen area as a peddler hawking goods from his base in Cleveland. Charlie married a local girl, Blanche Westmoreland, and went on to become Helen's leading citizen until his retirement in the 1950s.

Charlie Maloof (on the left) and Frank Barrett enjoy refreshments and a game of cards.

The old Unicoi Road was improved with the addition of bridges over the Chattahoochee below Nora Mills and in the center of Helen. Along with the train came telegraph and telephone service. The phones at the mill and Mountain Ranch were private, but everyone had access at Lawrence Vandiver's drugstore. Children who ran messages about town were sometimes rewarded with sums as large as a nickel for their trouble.

Ice could also be had at the drugstore; it came up from Gainesville on the train to be stored in a cooler, or "ice-house". Helen got electricity, courtesy of a steam-driven generator at the mill. However, the lights would begin to blink every evening at 9:55, reminding residents that it would be "lights out" at 10 o'clock when the generator was shut down.

People came from all over to work at the mill or participate in a supporting enterprise in the new town. Helen's first mayor was R.O. Byars, superintendent of the mill and a former resident of St. Louis. The first baby born in the new town was the daughter of Mr. and Mrs. E.W. Mead, "recent arrivals from LosAngeles, California". Although local men got their share of jobs, they had to compete with more experienced hands who followed the sawmills to new locations as America's virgin forests were depleted in the East.

POSING ON MAIN STREET, in front of the Helen barber shop in 1926. The little girl is Billie Adams (Brown), who grew up to teach for many years in local schools. Beside her are Arnold McCollum (barber at the time), Hubert Allen, Grover Cagle, and Jim Westmoreland. Hubert and Jim were mechanics in the garage next door which remained in business for 50 more years, eventually being run by Jim's brother "Chief" Westmoreland and remodeled in the Alpine style. The woman standing on the left is Creed Allen Hooper. The other woman is Glenn Puett Adams, Billie's mom. Billie's parents ran the cafe just on the other side of the garage, where the family lived in a room in the back.

Byrd-Matthews Lumber Co.   Helen, Georgia.   (Capacity, 125,000 feet per day.)

BYRD-MATTHEWS/MORSE BROTHERS MILL. *Helen's mill was one of the largest east of the Mississippi. When both bandsaws were running, capacity was 125,000 board feet per day. The mill was entirely self-sufficient since it was powered with scrap wood from the cutting operations. Most of the mill was disassembled and shipped to Mexico when operations ceased in 1931.*

THE GREAT SAWMILL

*H*elen's huge sawmill was actually two mills in one, for when it was in full operation, two long metal bands ran side by side, screaming in stereo as they cut into the prime virgin wood brought from the mountains. The sawyers rode back and forth on carriages with the logs they were cutting. As cut boards fell from the carriages, they were conveyed out of the mill via a "pretty clever" distribution system and stacked down the valley to dry before being shipped out on the trains of the G.& N.W.R.R.

The entire sawmill operation was self-sufficient. Waste wood from the cutting operations was used to power the steam boilers housed in a separate building which sported five tall smokestacks. When logs came in on the train, they were dumped into a pond in front of the mill and floated over to the large conveyor which lifted them up into the mill. Floating the heavy logs not only made them easy to handle, but also served to wash off some of the mud they had acquired while being drug across the forest floor.

From Helen, rails were laid into the mountains where temporary camps were established to house the loggers and railroad workers. Since the work was hard and the camps offered minimal comforts, they tended to attract what were locally referred to as "wood hicks": rough, coarse men of the woods who had little in the way of education and social skills. The Helen policeman and the County sheriff stayed busy as the wood hicks often resorted to fists, knives or guns when disagreement arose. When they came to town on weekends to get their paychecks and a jar of moonshine liquor, Helen was a wild and sometimes dangerous place.

Barbara Anderson recorded an eye-witness account relayed by Garland Vandiver describing a Helen evening during this time:

I remember one incident that... fortunately wound up on the humorous side... one man resented another man's attention to his wife and, being pretty well inebriated, pulled out his gun. The threatened man tried to protect himself by hiding behind the door leading into the room in which the party was taking place. However, the area behind the door was not safe enough and he was shot. The bullet fortunately just grazed his head, leaving it somewhat gory and bloody. He slumped to the floor with fright and the man who had done the shooting, figuring he had really done himself in, flew thru the door and was never seen in these parts again. The man who was shot stumbled out of the house and as he passed another member of the party who had somewhat passed out by the side of the house, he cried, "I'm shot, I'm shot!" His nearby audience was heard to mutter somewhat dazedly, "That's nothing -- I'm half shot!"

The first areas to be cut were on the headwaters of the Chattahoochee River. Although things got off to a fast start, Byrd-Matthews ran into difficulties by 1917. They last worked on Smith Creek above today's Unicoi State Park. With the Smith Creek valley blocked by Anna Ruby Falls, it was necessary to slide timber over the falls and through the adjoining gorge to reach the logging trains waiting about a half mile below. Local accounts say so much timber was splintered as it "ballhooted" over slides constructed at the falls that Byrd-Matthews went broke. However, it also appears that falling timber prices caused some of their difficulties.

In 1917, the Morse Brothers Lumber Company out of Rochester New York acquired the great mill. For the next 14 years, Morse Brothers succeeded where Byrd-Matthews had not. Operations proceeded over to Dukes Creek and nearly 20 miles further west, all the way over into Blood Mountain Cove in neighboring Lumpkin County. When these areas were cut, a new line was built to the east, running about 40 miles from Helen past Lake Burton and on up the headwaters of the Tallulah River nearly to the North Carolina line. A poplar tree cut on the Tallulah River measured 7 feet across at the base; part of the opening for the conveyor at the mill had to be torn away to admit this huge log.

In an essay written for the White County Historical Society, Charles White recalled the day Helen's big mill closed down:

Morse Brothers sawed their last board at Helen on May 5, 1931. At two o'clock in the afternoon of that day, the head of steam in the boilers was released by the whistle, which blew for thirty minutes, and when its echoes died out among the mountains, an era in White County died too.

Wood hicks were replaced by "good-byes" on the streets of Helen as many left to follow the jobs elsewhere. Except for the boilers, most of the

sawmill was dismantled and shipped to Mexico, where operations were interrupted first by a flood and then by the gunfire of a revolution which sent many mill workers packing. However, this was a temporary setback for Morse Brothers, which is still headquartered in Rochester, NY and still in the lumber business today.

In the single most important event to shape the modern mountain landscape, the US Forest Service arrived in the 1920s to begin acquiring most of the cut-over lands.

Sawmilling continued in the area after the great mill was gone, but scattered small sawmills took the place of the large and dramatic operation which had been in Helen.

Trucks replaced trains as the age of steam came to an end. Unfortunately, the mill left just as the Great Depression arrived, leaving Helen to suffer through some lean times.

TANNIC ACID PLANT. In 1923, the Smethport Extract Company of Virginia constructed this acid plant in the river bottoms just above the present entrance to the Alpine Crest Resort; the old concrete pillars standing there are all that remain of the facility. Using the rails of the sawmill to bring chestnut and hemlock logs from the mountains, the bark was processed to produce tannic acid used for making leather. The operation lasted only about five years before financial difficulties forced its closure. In 1928, the Forest Service obtained much of Smethport's mountain holdings for inclusion in the new National Forest.

Nacoochee Station (Gainesville and Northwestern Railway).   Nacoochee Valley, Georgia.

NACOOCHEE STATION. Train stations along the line of the G.&.N.W.R.R. were not fancy; after being cut in half and turned sideways, the Nacoochee Station still stands beside the Highway 75 bridge at the upper end of Nacoochee Valley.

THE GAINESVILLE AND NORTHWESTERN RAILROAD

When the train steamed into White County, it was cause for celebration, for a long-awaited event had finally occurred. White Countians had been clamoring for a railroad for years, especially after seeing the benefits neighboring Habersham County enjoyed when they got a local line in the 1880s. The *Cleveland Courier* boldly predicted that mines, agriculture, and tourism would flourish as the age of prosperity had at last arrived.

The use of "Northwestern" in the name is a bit curious, since the line actually ran northeast rather than northwest. However, the Missourians who built it came from the northwest. The name suited them and, since it was their railroad, they simply chose a name they liked without apparent regard to actual geographic considerations.

The railroad was necessary for the sawmill, and, as things turned out, when the mill left, the railroad wasn't far behind. Although there were many riders at first, "Daily Double Passenger Service" was cut in half in less than four years. Local mines turned out asbestos and an auxiliary line hauled copper ore from a mine in Lumpkin County, but as these operations declined it was also becoming apparent that the anticipated booms in tourism and agriculture were not happening either.

The tracks of the G.&.N.W.R.R. were not first-rate to begin with, but in its later years the cash-strapped railroad was beset by so many derailments that a shorthand message was devised to report incidents: after climbing a telephone pole with a portable phone, a crewman would call the main office in Gainesville to simply say: "Off again, on again, gone again." In the final years, passenger service was provided by buses on railroad wheels, one of which was known as the "Yellow Hammer".

LEAVING NACOOCHEE. *Just out of the Nacoochee Station, this passenger train is coming up the tracks across the river from Nora Mills, where the old roadbed remains undisturbed.*

The railroad came to a land of wagons and mules, but it was soon competing with automobiles, trucks and bus lines for business. When the mill left Helen, the G.&.N.W.R.R. began retreating towards Gainesville. Trains still came to Cleveland in 1935, but by 1936, the rails were removed and White County's railroad was gone. Among the things Helen residents lost was the ice the train had supplied; those lucky enough to have automobiles had to make trips to nearby Clarkesville to fill the ice-house.

1930s MAIN STREET. The field in the foreground was used as a common pasture; Billy Adams Brown remembers walking the family milk cow over in the morning and returning for it in the evening. However, this future school teacher didn't like milking, so she came up with a plan: after setting up to milk, Billy would give the cow a good pinch, causing it to turn over the milk bucket and her daddy to relieve her of the chore. The Helen baseball team also played in the pasture. Helen's train station is across the River in the left-hand side of the picture.

THE QUIET YEARS

*J*obs had never been plentiful in the mountains, but when the mill left and the Depression arrived, things were especially tough. Not everyone was affected in quite the same way, though. Traditional residents were in better shape if they still had the mule and smokehouse to rely on. Those who had come in to work at the mill had a harder time since they could not turn back to the farm, but even in the big city of Helen, chicken houses, pig-pens, and barns stood behind many houses. During the day, the livestock was taken to graze in the large pasture between the Mountain Ranch Hotel and the River.

Down at the Bank of Helen, it was a struggle, but under Charlie Maloof's management every depositor who asked got his money back. Moonshining helped many get by. The newly

"By God and by Sears and Roebuck we are going to make it!" was the saying during the dark days of the Great Depression. However, things were a little easier for local families who still had the means to practice traditional self-sufficient farming. And there were still plenty of mules around; Gene Burke stands atop this one.

arrived Forest Service supplied a few jobs. The government also helped out in 1933 with a Civilian Conservation Corps Camp ("CCC Camp") located where Unicoi State Park is today. Men from other regions were first employed at the camp; local men were hired later.

CCC jobs were highly prized and men like Smith Crumley came home to simply turn their entire paychecks over to their kinfolks. Among other projects, the CCC boys built or improved the present day Forest Service roads on the head of the Chattahoochee and Tray Mountain and constructed the first Chimney Mountain Road (now GA 356) running eastward past Unicoi towards Batesville and Lake Burton.

CIRCLE MILL. *When Morse Brothers left town, much of their Helen property was acquired by Charlie Maloof. The big mill was gone, but the building which housed the boilers remained to form the basis for a much smaller operation first run by Charlie and Mr. Miller. Providing much needed jobs, this mill operated until destroyed in a huge fire in the early 1950s.*

DOGWOOD SHUTTLE MILL. *The smallest of Helen's several timber operations was T.J. Tallant's mill which cut "shuttle blanks" from hard, durable dogwood. The blanks were shipped out to be turned on lathes and cut into shuttles (large spools) used by the textile industry. The mill operated from 1936 until the early 1960s. From left to right, the first man is unknown but the next three are Willard Tallant, T.J. Tallant and Hubert Martin.*

In the Helen valley, Charlie Maloof acquired most of the property sold by the departing Morse Brothers, including the remaining facilities where the great mill had been. Charlie and Charles Miller, former general manager for Morse Brothers, opened a mill on the site; it was a much smaller operation, but under various operators provided local employment for two decades. The Mountain Ranch Hotel continued in operation, offering popular Saturday night dances and one-armed bandits (supposedly "for amusement only") for entertainment.

Surprisingly, gold mining again became a source of employment when the government officially raised the price of gold by 70% in 1933. W.G. Hudson rebuilt the old Hamby Mining Ditch of J.R. Dean; Hudson's washing operations on the hills above Dukes Creek were successful until gold mining was halted by World War II. Overlooking Helen, the Franco-American Gold Mining Company burrowed into the side of Hamby Mountain, but hard rock mining proved less successful as they closed with a loss.

During the years the Franco-American mine operated, their assay office was established in the old post office, whose operations were temporarily moved down to the store of Verge Adams. The shift caused partisan rancor as Charlie Maloof and Will White, both ardent Democrats, became greatly chagrined since Verge Adams was a Republican, an affiliation he had acquired while growing up on the backside of the Blue Ridge in that over-mountain region where most of the few white Georgia Republicans of that era could be found.

COUNTRY STORE. Walt Sims stands in front of the store first operated by Verge Adams in the 1930s. At the time, this is where local residents paid their Georgia Power bills. Betty Fain's Country Store opened here in the 1970s before moving to its present site.

Those familiar with Helen in the 70s and 80s will remember this store building as the original location of Betty's Country Store. Adam's Store was also the place where electricity bills were paid when the lines of Georgia Power finally reached Helen.

During the 1930s, the old Unicoi Road was replaced with a new route built by State crews using convict labor. The present concrete bridge in downtown Helen was dedicated in 1939. However, the road was not paved for another decade. When the formal commemoration of the new asphalt was over, the real dedication took place: Jean Chastain and other Helen children took to the new and incredibly smooth pavement with their roller skates, suffering only an occasional interruption from a passing car.

DEDICATING THE BRIDGE. Formal lobbying efforts started in 1923, when a "Go To Helen" highway meeting was attended by citizens of Cleveland, Hiawassee, and Hayesville, NC who banded together to form the "Nacoochee-Hiawassee Scenic Highway Association". Will White, the man standing in the picture, was elected president. Besides advocating a modern highway to replace the old Unicoi Road to Hiawassee and Hayesville, the association was to advertise the cities along the way and "perpetuate the Indian legends of this section". It took 15 years, but by 1938 the present day concrete bridge in downtown Helen was complete and State highway crews were working to the north. Seated on the first row are "Dandy" Vandiver who sold the land where the Byrd-Matthews sawmill was located, Charles Miller who formed a partnership with Charlie Maloof to operate the "circle mill" after the big mill left, and Charlie Maloof himself, who peers around Will White's elbow.

CHANGING VIEWS ON MAIN STREET. In the first picture, taken in about 1915 from a vantage point near the old iron bridge, the Mountain Ranch Hotel stands on the hill, poles support electric and phone wires, and Main Street offers a public well. When the present concrete bridge was built in 1938, the road was moved over, giving old downtown Helen a triangle-shape which still shows today. In the 1950s picture, the road is paved and the Hotel gone, although the dance pavillion survives. Comparing these pictures to the ones on pages 8 and 49 shows changes from Helen's earliest days to Alpine times.

By the 1940s, the Helen Post Office had been returned to its rightful place downtown, leaving Charlie Maloof and Will White free to get their mail without partisan discord. A fixture of Helen life was the loud steam-whistle at the sawmill, which blew every work-day at 8AM, noon, and finally at 5PM, when children would know to go home. Since everyone knew the mail truck from Gainesville would stop by shortly after the morning whistle and then, after proceeding to Hayesville, NC and back, stop once again in the late afternoon, morning and evening gatherings at the Post Office joined the shrieks of the whistle in framing the day's communal activities.

Helen's economy suffered two hard blows after World War II. In 1945, the Mountain Ranch Hotel burned to the ground. In the early 1950s, the sawmill which Charlie Maloof and Mr. Miller had first operated was also destroyed in a huge fire. John Anderson recalls that stacks of drying lumber added considerably to the searing blaze, which toppled the old smokestacks erected by Byrd-Matthews forty years before and left melted coke bottles among the ashes of Helen's original industry.

THIRTY YEARS OF GRACIOUS HOSPITALITY came to an end when the Mountain Ranch Hotel burned in 1945. The adjoining dance pavillion survived to continue as the scene of local gatherings for many years.

HELEN BASEBALL TEAMS. *Helen's first team was sponsored by the sawmill and quit playing when it closed down. Bill Elrod, first on the left/ back row of the 1930 picture, came up from Lavonia, GA in 1919 to play for Morse Brothers. The ball field was in a large pasture between the River and Pete's Park (which now sits atop the hill in the background of the 1951 picture); this pasture was also home to the 9-hole golf course of the Mountain Ranch Hotel. Both activities co-existed with the cattle which grazed there during the day. The Helen club was re-organized in the early 1950s under manager Bill Elrod, who returned to the diamond over thirty years after he'd come to play ball and is the only man in both pictures. Games against neighboring towns drew large and enthusiastic crowds; opponents included the black team from neighboring Bean Creek and teams from Blairsville, Clarkesville, Cleveland, Hayesville, NC and the textile mills at Gainesville. Members of the 1951 team were: (front) Neal Ash, Ross Cathy, Grover Cagle, Bud Beachum, Ted Brown, Bobby Russell, Claude Bristol; (back) Lee Mize, Paul Brock, Wilburn Burke, Hugh Dorsey Williams, Tom Pardue, Bo Benton, manager Bill Elrod, and team organizer Major Dorsey.*

All the news was not bad, though. As already recounted, it was during this same period that Jimmy Wilkins arrived to make hosiery and, later, women's apparel at Orbit Manufacturing. Helen's fortunes also improved when Unicoi State Park opened in 1954 and the sale of beer and wine was approved a few years after that.

READY WILCO. *Jimmy Wilkins stands in the middle of the picture, taken during the 1950s at the Wilco Hosiery Mill in downtown Helen. Seeking a place to set up shop with equipment he had acquired in Canada, Jimmy looked first in nearby Cleveland before deciding to locate in Helen when Charlie Maloof promised to construct a building for his factory. Although Jimmy did not realize it at the time and still does not believe it, there is otherwise universal agreement that his first home in Helen was actually a train station: he lived in the remodeled depot of the old Gainesville and Northwestern Railroad before moving downriver to build a modern home with adjoining golf course in a bottom area where the houses of mill workers once stood.*

COMMERCIAL HOTEL. *One of several hotels and boarding houses which served mill workers, the Commercial Hotel was a wild place when the "wood hicks" came to stay on weekends. By some accounts, women of an agreeable, but business-like, nature also inhabited the hotel when the wood hicks were there. During the week, these ladies worked around town as domestics, but let it be known that they would not be available for such chores on weekends. In addition to the ladies of the Commercial Hotel, early Helen offered bootleg whiskey, a pool hall, and a small bowling alley for holiday diversions. In its later years the Hotel was home to the Helen switchboard and Floyd Caudell, who manned the phones for years after suffering a disabling auto accident. Floyd's niece Lillian Mauldin also helped out; she is pictured at the switchboard. When Helen parents wanted their children to come home, the phone would ring with a request for Floyd to send them that way. Always a "jolly fellow", Floyd also enjoyed the company of adults, as the inset picture shows.*

Although the coming of the hosiery mill meant jobs, it did cause worry from an unexpected quarter. When some locals were heard to say that a regular paycheck would let them quit moonshining, E. L. "Ed" Gedney, the somewhat mischievous proprietor of Escowee Rabbitry, expressed concern that the supply of liquor might be adversely impacted. He needn't have worried, though, as stills and whisky runners stayed busy for years. Even today, bootleg whisky is readily available for those who know where to look.

Although it wasn't as dramatic, the appearance of Helen did change in the years before the Alpine conversion. Outhouses, including the ones sitting out over the river, slowly faded from the scene. In the early 50s, committees were formed to plant dogwoods and flowers along Main Street. As the improvement effort continued, attention turned to the chicken houses, pig-pens and barns which still stood behind many houses; these, too, slowly disappeared.

As 1960 approached, Ed Gedney, former proprietor of Escowee Rabbitry and future mayor of Helen, embarked on a clean-up campaign of his own. Jean Chastain and Ethyl Cagle recall that when Ed and wife Dot opened the "Laun-Dry-Eze" with its coin-operated washers and dryers, the town was improved in another way as women took down "curtains and everything else" which had been too much trouble to run through their old-fashioned wringers and cleaned them for the first time.

Continuing the theme, E.L. acquired the old Commercial Hotel where the Helen switchboard had been and added pay showers. However, even though showers were still close to a novelty for many residents, public bathing was much less successful than public laundering.

By the 1960s, most homes sprouted antennas to catch a weak signal from distant TV stations in Atlanta, and maybe even Chattanooga if the receiver could be placed high enough on the hill. The federal government arrived to build a housing project in the field where the Helen baseball teams had once played.

Helen's hamburger joint, the "Ice-Burg", was a classic drive-in scene and evening gathering place for the young, and one where Doris Ruth Cathy could relay with great character all of the latest news (to call it gossip would be a great injustice), if you hadn't already heard it from Lois Brown down at Warren's Chevron Station (they had groceries too).

Almost everyone who lived in Helen during the "quiet years" expresses fond memories of those times. They remember things like the day Beulah Adams died during one of the prettiest spring-time snows, which unfortunately put the power out. Smith Crumley went about the darkened town collecting all the old lanterns to light the Adams place, where most in the community came by to support as best they could. And as John Anderson said of childhood in old Helen, "nobody had it better", in a place where kids were free to roam and most of the older folks were assigned the honorary title of "aunt" or "uncle" whether they were blood kin or not.

END OF AN ERA. This picture of the inside of Warren Brown's gas station and grocery store was taken shortly before Helen's Alpine conversion. Although the solitary figure might appear lonely, the "loafers benches" around the stove were often the stage for story tellers and lively conversation among the members of a close-knit community. News traveled fast as just about everyone passed through at least one of the town's several such stores in the course of a day. Unfortunately, traditional Helen could not survive the crowds and rising land prices brought by the Alpine Village. Like the out-houses and barns of Helen's earlier days, the scene at the loafer's benches was left to fade away in the new scheme of things.

Helen Presbyterian
Built and dedicated in 1927

*C*HURCHES.   Helen is home to three churches, all of which welcome Sunday visitors. The Holiness congregation first met in a tent and then upstairs in a downtown store before building their present RIVERSIDE WORSHIP CENTER some years ago. Their church is located on River Street, in the main part of town.

The HELEN PRESBYTERIAN CHURCH was organized in 1927, when the frame building pictured above was built. The church had a somewhat unusual beginning, since the charter members included "Methodists, Baptists, Lutherans, Dutch Reformed, and one Presbyterian, Miss Edwards". However, this assortment was about right for Helen, which at the time was a mixture of sawmill outsiders of various faiths and local mountaineers, virtually all of whom were Baptists or Methodists. The Presbyterians' current brick building replaced the old frame structure in 1952. This church is located on Main Street near Betty's Store.

During the period of early Alpine zeal, artist John Kollock produced an ornate sketch for converting the Presbyterian Church to the bavarian style, but they declined the suggestion. It remained for the Baptists to endorse the Alpine theme, for when they built HELEN FIRST BAPTIST CHURCH, it was done in bavarian style. Having grown quickly to become Helen's largest, this church sits above Main Street across from the Super 8 Motel and the Days Inn.

Helen Schools Opens Monday

School will begin at Helen Junior High School Monday, Sept. 2 at 9 o'clock. It is hoped that every child of school age will be present on the first day in order that no time will be lost in getting the work started for a successful year.

All patrons are urged to be present on the opening day. The faculty is the same as last year. Miss Mellie Reed, of Oakwood, principal; Miss Olean Vandiver, Helen, teacher of grammar school department: Miss Irene Reed, Oakwood, teacher of intermediate department, and Miss Mary Ray, of Maysville, will have charge of primary department.

Cleveland Courier 8/30/29

*H*ELEN SCHOOLS. Helen had its own school until county buses arrived in the early 1960s. Generations of children had teachers like Miss Sullivan, Conie Brooks, and the ladies listed in the article above. The old wooden school was located where the Chattahoochee Motel now stands; part of the facility remains as the motel office. A water fountain stood out front; it was at this very fountain that Leigh Gedney applied a joy-buzzer to the posterior of Blanch Burke, causing the loss of a tooth. Behind, his-and-hers outhouses stood over the river, allowing their occupants to peer down through the portals to see large catfish swimming in the icy waters of the Chattahoochee. The building was also used for church services and movies were shown there during the depression years when the boys from the CCC camp would come to town. Built across the river after WWII, the newer cement-block structure later became the site of Orbit Manufacturing Company.

***Laurel Thicket or Rhododendron Hell?**   Since both have dark foliage and distinctive gnarled limbs, it's easy to get these two mountain trademarks confused. The laurel (above)has elliptical, pointed leaves and bunches of flowers that look like tiny parachutes. Different kinds of mountain rhododendrons bloom white, pink, or purple, but all have leaves shaped like those of the magnolia.*

CHAPTER 5: WILDER PLACES

UNICOI STATE PARK is located on Smith Creek three highway miles north of Helen. When it was dedicated in 1954, then-governor Herman Talmadge said there would have been no park without Charlie Maloof. Back when the old "county-unit system" favored acres over population in determining representation at the statehouse, rural leaders had more opportunity for influence than their modern counterparts. But if the possibility was there, it still took an opportunist to make things happen, and it was Charlie who conceived the notion of the park and headed the effort to push it through.

With the addition of hundreds of acres of forest land in the 1970s, Unicoi's boundary now extends to the Helen city limits. A hiking trail departing from the Helen Library/Pete's Park area winds through the woods for two miles to Unicoi Lodge and from there six miles further to Anna Ruby Falls.

The focus of the park is a beautiful 53 acre lake nestled deep in the valley of Smith Creek where the soaring ridges of Tray Mountain rise abruptly on either side as dramatic backdrops. Although the dam originally took less than two years to construct, the lake was drained in the early 1990s for repairs which took over five years to complete. During this period, the state Natural Resources Commissioner continually maintained the delays were due to the weather, even though there were several droughts and two presidential elections during the supposed wet spell. However, it's also true that the old county-unit system was gone and there was no local leader like Charlie Maloof who took an interest in the situation.

73

Unicoi was operated as a traditional park until 1968, when notions of innovation in government gave control to the semi-independent North Georgia Mountains Authority. During five years under the Authority, in keeping with the Great Society spirit of the times, federal funds were obtained and the park remodeled with 84 new campsites, a second swimming area with an adjacent "trading post", 25 rental cabins, the imaginative "Squirrel's Nest" group camping area consisting of shelters stacked in a laurel thicket on the side of a hill, and a 60-room lodge of unique design.

The award winning lodge has since been renovated and enlarged to 100 rooms with conference facilities for up to 400 people. The lodge also has a buffet-style restaurant and the **Mountain Craft Shop** specializing in handcrafted items, quilts and books. Xavier Roberts, proprietor of Babyland General and creator of the Cabbage Patch dolls, supported himself by selling pottery in this shop and working as a Unicoi crafts counselor while developing his now-famous concept of soft-sculpture dolls with individual birth certificates.

Under the Mountains Authority, Unicoi was also a research station which promoted the idea that development was desirable as long as it was beneficial to traditional mountain residents and respected the land, a notion offensive enough for local members of the General Assembly to mandate that Unicoi be returned to operation as a traditional state park in 1973.

In the mid-1990s, the State decided it should not be in the business of running the lodges which it had spent 30 years building at various Georgia parks. In 1997, Unicoi was "privatized" and is now run by a commercial contractor on the theory that this will result in more efficient operations leading to profits for the State and better service for the visitor. Fortunately, through all of the changes, Unicoi remains a beautiful spot, and visitors can again enjoy the charms of the lake.

*Utilizing an innovative Forest Service design, "**Barrel Cabins**" rest upon poles to minimize impacts on the forest floor.*

AWARD WINNING UNICOI LODGE today offers 100 rooms, conference facilities, a buffet-style restaurant and the Mountain Craft Shop specializing in hand-crafted items, quilts and books.

BUILDING THE TRAIL. *Forest Service workers near the end of the half-mile trail from the parking area to the falls.*

A **NNA RUBY FALLS.** This unusual double falls is at the confluence of York and Curtis Creeks, which are named for pioneer settlers who lived upstream. Capt. J. H. Nichols of Nacoochee named the falls themselves in honor of his only daughter when he acquired the site after the Civil War (coming nearly 50 years after the first settlers, Nichols did not "discover" the falls as it's sometimes said). In 1916, the Byrd-Matthews Lumber Company suffered considerable losses in trying to slide logs past the falls and through the gorge below. From the base of the falls down to Robertstown, the merged stream is known as Smith Creek, retaining the name applied by the original Georgia surveyor in 1819. The Anna Ruby parking area is reached by driving to Unicoi State Park and following the park road around the west side of the lake and on up Smith Creek. From there, a half-mile paved trail to the falls departs from the **Gift Shop/Visitor's Center** run by the **Chattahoochee-Oconee Heritage Association.** Several species of trillium join other native wildflowers along the trail in the spring. Visitors can feed the large trout which reside in the pool below the observation deck at the gift shop. A trail for the visually impaired and ι stream-side picnic area are also located beside the parking lot.

MARTIN MINE/REYNOLDS VEIN. This is the largest vein working in the Helen area. Ore from the vein was crushed with a 20-stamp mill powered with water from the Hamby Ditch. Although this hole at the surface is small, the shaft opens up into a huge room which disappears below the water line. The Martin Mine Trail leads through this cut.

*D*UKES CREEK CONSERVATION AREA /SMITHGALL WOODS.
After graduating from Georgia Tech in 1933, Charles Smithgall went on to make a sizeable fortune during a 50-plus year career in radio and newspapers, which included ownership of the old WRNG AM in Atlanta ("Ring Radio"), the Gainesville Times, and half of the Gwinnett Daily News (which he sold for $50 million in 1987). In 1983, he began acquiring considerable acreage along Dukes Creek, the Chattahoochee tributary which runs through the large valley just west of Helen, causing speculation that he would develop a resort or "Six Flags Over Helen" sort of attraction.

However, Smithgall soon put such notions to rest when he announced his intention to return the land to its natural state, saying "...they may have had a good idea with the resort -- make it a resort for deer and bear!" He had picked a challenging site, for, in addition to the usual logging, large portions of the

Dukes Creek valley had been turned upside down and washed away in over a century of gold mining. Although the destruction of the American Chestnut by an imported blight precludes a true restoration to pre-logging times, estimates are that the land can return to an approximation of its original state in 200-300 years.

After a decade of effort, which required a lot of lawyerly work to clear titles which had been mixed-up since the Gold Rush, Smithgall eventually acquired nearly 6000 acres stretching from the Helen city limits to the boundary of the National Forest. To maintain his legacy, Smithgall sought a buyer willing to preserve the land. Under Governor Zell Miller's Preservation 2000 Program, the State acquired the site in 1994, designating it as a Heritage Preserve to ensure maximum legal protection.

Although protection and restoration remain primary goals, limited recreational use is also encouraged. Private vehicles are prohibited, but shuttle service and guided tours are available on Wednesdays and weekends. With 12 miles of mostly unpaved roads, Smithgall Woods is probably the best place in northeast Georgia for mountain cycling. Easy routes along Dukes Creek are complicated only by two fords (peddlers' feet will go underwater) and an occasional wild turkey, but it takes a hardy biker to peddle over Hamby Mountain. The newest addition to a growing network of hiking trails is the historic Martin Mine Trail, which leads through the largest hard-rock mining site in the Helen area.

For groups, the Woods offers a conference center with overnight accommodations, environmental education classes, the Bear Ridge primitive group camp, and a covered picnic shelter. The Conservation Area is open for quota hunts during the season; for safety reasons, most other activities are curtailed during these times. The preserve is open year-round for catch-and-release trout fishing with barbless hooks. However, only 15 anglers at a time are allowed during sessions on Wednesdays and weekends; the number of sessions varies with the season and reservations are strongly recommended.

For reservations or more information on the Dukes Creek Conservation Area, stop by the **Visitor's Center** located at the intersection of Alternate 75 and the Russell Scenic Highway or call (706) 878-3087. A $2.00 parking fee is required, but there is no additional charge for programs or recreational activities. Hunting and fishing licenses are available at the Center, which also offers wildlife displays and refreshments.

JAUNTY CREW. *Enjoying an outing on the Appalachian Trail during the 1930s, this spirited group poses on the summit of Tray Mountain.*

*C*HATTAHOOCHEE NATIONAL FOREST/APPALACHIAN TRAIL. Given the extent of the modern Forest, it may seem hard to believe the government didn't own a single acre of woodlands in north Georgia before 1911. In the Helen area, large cut-over tracts purchased during the 1920s from Byrd-Matthews, Morse Brothers and Smethport Extract became the core of the present day Forest. When the lands were acquired, deer and trout were severely depleted and black bears all but extinct. In some areas, mountaineers deliberately burned 60% of the forest each year to encourage fresh spring growth for foraging livestock.

Although issues like wilderness and clear-cutting continue to cause controversy, the National Forest is one government program which has been very successful. Under joint state and federal management, today's forests yield a steady supply of timber while giving the public access to 750,000 acres of Georgia mountain land teeming with deer, bear, and constantly re-supplied with fish. Recreational use has greatly increased in recent years, forcing the Forest Service to limit use of some roads and camping areas.

The Forest Service road which traverses the Chattahoochee headwaters begins at the Chattahoochee Methodist Church in Robertstown and ends 14 miles later on GA 75 at Unicoi Gap. This road is closed at times during the winter months. The Tray Mountain road can be accessed on GA 75 a mile above Robertstown and via GA 356 three miles past Unicoi State Park. Roads are graveled and passable in all weather except winter snows. They are also narrow and very curvy in most places; slow speeds and caution are advised. Except for improved campgrounds at Andrews Cove on GA 75 above Helen and the Chattahoochee River Campground on the head of the river, camping is free in the Forest. Primitive campgrounds on the Chattahoochee headwaters may be full (and noisy) on summer weekends.

The first documented proposal for an *APPALACHIAN TRAIL* was a 1921 article by Benton MacKaye (spoken as if spelled "Ma-Kye" and rhyming with "sky"). As more Americans crowded into cities to labor in factories and offices, MacKaye and others concluded that maintaining "the ability to cope with nature directly -- unshielded by the weakening wall of civilization -- is one of the admitted needs of modern times." Seeing an opportunity, MacKaye proposed a trail to run along the mostly undeveloped peaks of the Appalachians.

More than a mere footpath, MacKaye's trail was intended to connect a series of alternative communities offering "a sanctuary and a refuge from the scramble of every-day commercial life." Small cooperatives along the trail would engage in "outdoor non-industrial endeavors" including agricultural, recreational, medical and educational activities. Residents would live in separate houses owned by the community, which would stay small and non-profit. MacKaye believed many afflicted with "tuberculosis, anemia, and insanity" could be cured if brought to the mountains, since what they needed was "acres not medicine."

MacKaye's utopian vision did not prevail, but with the participation of thousands of volunteers all along the Appalachians, the help of the U.S. Forest Service, and the formation of the Appalachian Trail Conference in 1925, the trail itself became a reality. The Georgia section was open by 1931, although land acquisitions to completely protect it were not finished until 1994. The **Georgia Appalachian Trail Club** (P.O. Box 654, Atlanta, GA 30301, 404/634-6495) maintains the 80 miles in Georgia; new members are welcome.

On the Trail, the "weakening wall of civilization" is ever more intrusive as cell-phones and hand-held satellite locators join the array of modern equipment deployed by modern hikers. Although some sojourners judge fellow travelers by the gear they carry, Benton MacKaye would feel right at home among the idealists and dreamers who also frequent the path. In the Helen area, Highway 75 out of Helen, the Richard Russell Scenic Highway, and US 129 out of Cleveland cross the Trail at the crest of the Blue Ridge.

RICHARD RUSSELL SCENIC HIGHWAY. Named for the revered Georgia senator who supported it in Washington, the Scenic Highway was dedicated in 1968. Like the proposed extension of the Blue Ridge Parkway into Georgia, it was opposed by the Forest Service and conservationists who considered both unnecessary gashes through the most remote sections of the Appalachian woods. Although the Parkway was stopped, opponents could only influence the route of the Russell Highway, which was blasted high along the side of the mountain rather than beside the banks of Dukes and Dodd Creeks as many proponents preferred. The route was probably a good compromise, for the "Scenic" (as it's referred to locally) offers both sweeping vistas and connections to footpaths leading to the undisturbed settings of **DUKES CREEK FALLS** and the **RAVEN CLIFFS**, an unusual split rock formation housing two waterfalls and a rare vertical "chimney" through which an incautious tourist can take a 50 foot plunge. After climbing to nearly 3500 feet at Hogpen Gap, the Scenic passes through Tesnatee Gap to follow the general path of the old Logan Turnpike down into Union County. Where the Scenic starts, the rhododendrons bloom white and Eastern Cottontails hop about, but purple rhododendrons and New England Cottontails join other northern species on the ridges at the top of the mountain, which can be visited via the **APPALACHIAN TRAIL**. The road was the notion of James P. Davidson, long-time publisher of the *Cleveland Courier*, who is pictured above with Senator Russell near Hogpen Gap as the highway nears completion.

PICTURE/EXHIBIT INDEX AND CREDITS

* White County Historical Society
** Sautee-Nacoochee Community Association
*** Georgia Department of Archives and History

ACKNOWLEDGMENTS

First, some disclaimers: Everyone sees things a little differently, and this is simply my best effort at recounting the history of a place to which I am strongly attached. I apologize in advance for any factual errors, knowing that there are always at least a few (let me know and I'll try to fix them if there is a second printing). And this is by no means the whole story of Helen. Even though it's a small place, it's been the scene of enough human dramas so that another writer would have doubtless encountered and chosen other tales and people to include.

I do hope not to have left anyone out of the following acknowledgments (if I did, let me know and I'll try fix that if there is a second printing). I've listened for years to my father, Leigh Gedney, and at length to Billy Adams Brown, both of whom attended Helen's old wooden school in the 1930s; this writing is dedicated to them. Billy has long since become Helen's foremost archivist, collecting photographs, articles, memories and just about anything else that relates to the town. She also pretty much insisted this volume be written, and it may not be enough. Thanks to: Michael Humphries for advice on publishing. For suggesting the format and general ongoing feedback, to my wife Cindy Gedney and mother Catherine Gedney. For sharing or taking photographs, to Billy, Alva Kimsey and Gary Reese, Mary Henderson Davidson, Gene Burke, Roy Sims, Warren Brown, Dr. Tom Lumsden, Sarah Gillespie Fenner, Anna Cook, Fannie Lusk, Shirley Black McDonald, Garrison and Susan Baker, Page Gedney, David Greear, Hugh Elrod and the White County Historical Society, and particularly to Mike Wilkins for collecting many of them around Helen. For use of their paintings, to Ken Woodall and Donna Myers.

For much help with editing photographs and especially for the cover, to David Greear. Special thanks to Catherine Gibbs Gedney for spending many hours scanning the numerous photographs and sending them over the Internet. I've talked to many folks over the years, but for sharing memories especially for this effort, thanks to Fannie Vandiver Lusk, Comer Vandiver, John and Paulette Anderson, Kermit Dye, Marion Williams, Sol Greear, Jean Chastain, Ethyl Cagle, Jimmy Wilkins, Mike Wilkins, Dr. Tom Lumsden, Judy Lovell, Shirley McDonald, Hugh Elrod and Mervin Fried. Thanks to Judy Presley and John Anderson for permission to use an excerpt from "Memories of Helen". For proofreading, many thanks to Ina Lashley and Isabel Couch. And a tip of the hat to writers like "Scoop" Scruggs, Garrison Baker, Dr. Tom Lumsden, Barbara Anderson/Garland Vandiver, Shirley McDonald, Mildred Greear, Phil Garner, and those long-time editors of the Cleveland Courier Alex and James P. Davidson for producing writings which are invaluable resources for everyone.

LIVING ON THE UNICOI ROAD

Picture by Ken Woodall

An epic account of Georgia frontier life and the great Georgia Gold Rush, ***Living On The Unicoi Road*** begins at a long-abandoned and all-but-forgotten pioneer cemetery and from there sets off on a 300-year odyssey through the Helen valley and across much of North Georgia. The region was the wild domain of panthers, Indians, traders, and soldiers for a hundred years until the Unicoi Turnpike was begun in 1813. The next century belonged to the pioneers and gold miners whose story is told for the first time in ***Unicoi Road***. The tale does not end there, though, for author Matt Gedney follows the threads of the past to find them still woven into the evolving tapestry of modern life in the beautiful northeast Georgia mountains.

WHAT OTHERS SAY: "Gedney weaves a captivating tale.... a most refreshing approach which blends the best of fact-based history with the charm of good old-fashioned Southern storytelling... a beautifully done work -- I read it twice within a few days!"   *D. Michael Allison, National Allison (Allanson) Family Association*

WHERE TO GET IT: For mail order, see the next page. ***Unicoi Road***   is available at most NE Georgia bookstores and many stores in the Helen area, the Helen Welcome Center, and the Dahlonega Gold Museum. In the Atlanta area, it can be found at Barnes and Noble. To order by phone and use a credit card, call Humpus Bumpus Bookstore in Cumming, Georgia @1-800-464-0683.

*View the **Unicoi Road Website** @ "www.mindspring.com/~littlestar/"*

MAIL ORDER FORM*

For a review of *Living on the Unicoi Road,* see the previous page. Shipping is $3.00 per order. Please send:

_____ copies of *LIVING ON THE UNICOI ROAD: Helen's Pioneer Century and Tales From the Georgia Gold Rush* @ $11.95 ea.

Subtotal $_____

_____ copies of *THE STORY OF HELEN AND THEREABOUTS* @ $8.95 ea.

Subtotal $_____

Shipping $ __3.00__

Total Amount $_____

My check or money order is enclosed. Please send to the following address:

NAME:_____

ADDRESS:_____

CITY: _____Zip_____

MAIL TO: Little Star Press
Dept. 214
175 Mt. Calvary Road
Marietta, GA 30064 U.S.A.

Thanks for your order!

*WHERE ELSE TO GET THEM: *Unicoi Road* and *Story of Helen* are available at most NE Georgia bookstores and selected stores in the Helen-Clarkesville-Gainesville area. In Atlanta, they can be found at Barnes and Noble and other selected stores. To order by phone and use a credit card, call Humpus Bumpus Bookstore in Cumming, Georgia @ 1-800-464-0683.

*Visit our **Website** @ "www.mindspring.com/~littlestar/"*